The Secr of a Righteous Black Woman
The Power of a Mother's Prayer

Learn How to Identify and Eliminate Fear and Negative Thinking Through Faith

INTERNATIONAL BESTSELLING AUTHOR
REEA RODNEY

Foreword by Dr. Janell Jones

**12 Inspirational Stories About a Mother's Unfailing Love
A Compilation with Other Dynamic Authors**

AN IMPRINT OF DARA PUBLISHING

ISBN: 978-1-7321362-4-3 (Paperback)
ISBN: 978-1-7321362-7-4 (eBook)
Library of Congress Control Number: 2021916296

Front cover image by Alexandra Gold
Book design by Kamaljeet Singh

Printed in the United States of America.

Disclaimer: The publisher and the authors do not make any guarantee or other promise as to any results that may be obtained from using the content of this book. This publication is meant as a source of valuable information for the reader, however it is not meant as a substitute for direct expert assistance. If such level of assistance is required, the services of a competent professional should be sought.

www.darapublishing.co

Dedication

This book is dedicated to all Black mothers—for always going beyond your natural abilities to love, care, provide for, protect, and nurture your children, in spite of all the adversities encountered, challenges faced, and fears experienced in the process of parenting your Black princes and princesses.

This anthology is a celebration of and a tribute to all Black mothers who Pray, Slay, and Always Find a Way.

You are Amazing. You are Strong. You are Beautiful.

Table of Contents

Other Books by the Author

Children's Storybooks

Juniper and Rose: Sisters First and Best Friends Forever
(English and Spanish)

Juniper and Rose: One More Bite Please (English and Spanish)

Juniper and Rose: We Will Come Back

Juniper and Rose Coloring and Activity Book (Volumes 1 & 2)

A Boy Name Tuck: Tuck and His Magical Stick

Empowerment Coaching Personal Development Workbooks for Kids

I Am Uniquely Made and Exceptionally Beautiful
Self-Esteem Workbook

I Am Fearless, Selfless and Destined for Greatness
Self-Confidence Workbook

I Am Who I Say I Am
Self-Talk Workbook

Standing in Our Greatness
Self-Love Workbook

If You Are Happy and You Know It Clap Your Hands
Self-Celebration Workbook

Bully Here, Bully There, Do You Care
Anti-Bullying Workbook

Children and Women Empowerment Journals

I Am Getting to Know Me Reflection Journal for Kids

Learning How to Empower Myself: A 12 Week Guide
Toward Self-Empowerment for Women

Self-Help & Motivational

I Empower Me – Mindfulness and Empowerment:
A Guide for Parents and Educators

Foreword

The stories within this inspired compilation resonate with me and all mothers. I can testify to the fears that come hand in hand, not just with parenting, but parenting in a world in crisis mode. Those who read these pages will, like me, gain valuable insight to overcome every fear and rise above.

Although each story is unique, they all intersect, featuring experiences we can all relate to. While the book presents practical solutions to win the battle with fear, it does so without minimizing the power of God to deliver us. On our parenting journey, as with all other endeavors, we must never lose sight of God. He has given us an avenue through prayer, whereby we can pour out our fears and complaints to Him and allow Him to relieve us of their burdens.

I'm convinced that there is no task more daunting than that of parenting. As your baby is placed in your hands for the very first time, you can't help but feel that tiny tremor of fear. It has been said, "With great power comes great responsibility." This saying holds true especially when it comes to parenting.

Having been specially elected by God—alongside fathers or, sometimes, separately—mothers are charged with the duty of not only nurturing and safeguarding their children but shaping them into God-fearing, respectable people. And while God has ably equipped us for the task, mentally we may question our abilities to do so, especially if we are being bombarded by fears.

The fears that we as Black mothers endure are not new. But they seem to grow as these age-old issues are regularly brought to the forefront. Our panoramic view of the world allows us to see the societal ills and injustices our children may fall prey to. They live in a world where their skin color makes them an easy target. As Black mothers, we have had to accept that some things are beyond our control. Nevertheless, we are compelled to do all that we can to shelter our children as we continue to yearn for a world where they can comfortably be themselves.

These fears don't go away once our children are older. As I parented, I naively thought that once my children crossed the threshold of adulthood, my worries about them would diminish. On the contrary, my concerns changed as they began to independently navigate their own lives, but they did not go away. I wanted to be sure my children made the best choices because I understood the importance of decision-making after my many failures. I wanted to do everything I could to spare them my same mistakes. But the truth was, I wasn't trusting God with my children.

I realized that there is only so much that we can do, and our helplessness feeds our fears. Even then, we are relentless in our efforts to provide a safety net for our kids, in the hopes that we can protect them from any potential misfortune. And although our rational mind tells us that this is literally impossible, it isn't enough to prevent us from trying.

While we may wish that our children could be spared some of the pain that we have known, we come to accept that they too must endure their own life trials. So, we live in fearful anticipation, knowing that inevitably the day will arrive when they will lose their innocence.

Parenting can be compared to a roller coaster ride—a series of ups and downs that can threaten to overwhelm as we are continually assailed by a battalion of emotions. Fear will be one of those emotions we will have to confront. Fear, like all other emotions, in and of itself is not bad. Like love, anger, or sadness, it serves as an indicator of our true feelings in the midst of our experiences, and it brings awareness of environmental triggers at work. Raw fear is instinctive.

Being fearful is nothing to be ashamed about. Sometimes our fears can be the most effective tool in our arsenal when protecting our children. Fears surrounding your children's well-being are normal and rational; however, if that fear overwhelms you to the point where it becomes debilitating, and you find yourself feeling defeated and doubting yourself as a parent, you may have to look at your fears from a different perspective. In that light, this book is an eye-opener.

As mothers, we nurture and guide our children. Part of that entails preparing them for every facet of the world—the good, the bad, and the ugly—and this can seem like a mammoth undertaking. If you are not mindful, your fears can morph into a "spirit of fear," which deflates and defeats. To guard against this, it's pivotal that we don't lose sight of God.

Remember that your relationship with Him is that of a father and his children. Believe it or not, He shares the very same concerns for us that we have for our kids. Therefore, we can draw comfort from knowing that He knows our limitations. He desires that we trust Him completely, casting our fears upon Him.

If we were to examine our fears, we would discover that they are not rooted in a lack of faith; we cry out to Him because we are confident in His power. Our doubts are really rooted in our inability to trust His plans.

We are unable to believe that all things will work together for our greater good, and therein lies our kryptonite. It weakens our defenses and renders us powerless to withstand the barrage of negative thoughts that attempt to steal our joy as mothers. We can rest assured that God does not want us to be laden with fears. He is bigger than all our worries, and He promises to strengthen us where we are weak. He will not leave us alone but will uphold us with His right hand.

He also urges us to not lean on our own understanding, but to acknowledge Him in all of our ways, and in return, He promises to direct our paths. We can surrender to Him, knowing that He is able to bear us up. Thankfully, prayer is the doorway through which we seek God, not only for the protection of our children, but for our own healing and deliverance, knowing that it is only through His grace that we can ever hope to be whole again.

This book offers twelve heartfelt prayers proven to be effective. Each author can attest to overcoming their fears after first surrendering them to God and then applying both Spirit-inspired and practical tools to the problem.

It is my sincere hope that this book will spark a revolution, as mothers all around the world will be empowered through its pages to challenge their fears and continue to tear down all negative stereotypes and labels that have been unfairly attached to our children. Join me and these authors in praying for our children—for they are how we change the world.

Dr. Janelle Jones
Licensed Clinical Therapist | Certified Life Coach
Motivational Speaker | International Bestselling Author

Preface

"And the LORD answered me, and said, Write the vision, and make it plain upon tables, that he may run that readeth it." Habakkuk 2:2

Time after time, I'm asked by my family, friends, and colleagues how I got the idea for my book. *Where did you get the inspiration?* To be completely honest, my response is always the same, for every book I write: "God." This is the most honest and sincere answer, and I always say it with such reverence and awe.

In the fall of 2015, while battling an illness, God whispered in my ear, "Write for your healing." At that time, I thought, *Write?* I never saw myself as a writer, and the idea seemed far-fetched. But I also thought I didn't have anything to lose, so I said to God, "Bring it on, baby!"

The very next year, I wrote and published my first children's book, and the following year, I published nine books—all thanks to the voice of God, who kept telling me what to write. I was also healed that year from a disease that has no cure, and I've learned to listen to God's voice and not question His instructions. I truly believe that is why He trusts me with these stories.

At the beginning of this year, 2021, I heard the voice of God again instructing me to write. Only this time, what He was requiring would cause me to step out of my comfort zone—something that I've gotten used to doing—and write about what seemed challenging to me.

You may be wondering what He asked me to write. Well, I heard God's voice, whispering, *"The Secret Prayer of a Righteous Woman: The Power of a Mother's Prayer."* Or so I thought. As I recited what I heard back to myself, the Holy Spirit corrected me, saying, "No, I said *The Secret Prayer of a Righteous Black Woman: The Power of a Mother's Prayer."*

And, to ensure that I understood what He wanted, the voice said, "Just like *Diary of a Mad Black Woman.*" I wasn't sure if I'd omitted it intentionally before, or if I hadn't heard Him correctly the first time, but I believe He wanted to emphasize that the word *Black* needed to come before *Woman.*

Right then and there, God chose the audience for this book: Black Mothers. He then told me that I was to write about the struggle I'd had the last year with my son wanting to purchase a car and the encounter I'd had with the police on January 4. I immediately thought, *Oh, no, God. Please don't tell me that You want me to write about racism, discrimination, and injustice toward people of color?*

Sure enough, that was what He wanted, but the book was also going to feature various fears that Black mothers have, although I couldn't understand why at that time. If I can be honest, I secretly rebelled at the thought of writing on the topic of racism. Probably I was scared of what others might think because I usually write about empowerment, personal development, and God. For as long as I could remember, scripture, politics, and racism were topics that I only explored deeply with a small, intimate circle of people. This was because I had seen and heard loud, tense, and disturbing debates over these subjects.

Now, here I had God telling me to write about the oppression, injustices, and fears that Black mothers were facing. I was afraid because I've always written books for everyone, and I always aimed to be inclusive in my work. Now, I was being instructed to write a book for Black mothers only. The writing was on the wall, and it was clear.

To see that I complied with His wishes, God took it a step further by involving my husband—I kid you not. He's a determined God, and He wants what He wants. But He also knows me as His daughter, and He knew I was struggling with His request. I wanted to be sure it was God who was talking to me. Fortunately, He called in reinforcements.

Remember that God can use anyone—you don't need a prestigious title or to be the bishop of a church. He uses the cast-out and forgotten, and

He also uses those who would never imagine themselves an instrument of honor to be used for noble purposes in His kingdom.

That night, when God gave me my mission with this book, He also shared with my husband some of the details, so that I could know it was Him and that this was what He wanted of me.

As I was about to share with my husband that God had spoken to me, my husband stopped me and said God had spoken to him too. I immediately asked, "What did He say?" He replied, "He showed me a silhouette of a woman praying." I began to scream as I felt the Holy Spirit descending upon me because God had shown me that very same image in a vision.

I also shared with my husband that God had showed me the color of the book cover. To my shock, he said God had showed him that too. I was astonished but at the same time not surprised by how God works. I said to my husband, "Don't tell me the color. Look it up on Google, and show it to me." I told him that I had something in that color, and I would show it to him at the same time.

My husband googled the color orange, and by that point, I was crying because it was the same color God showed me *and* the color of my jewelry case. I began to recite the words, "Speak, Lord, for thy servant heareth." There wasn't any doubt in my mind that He was talking to me.

God then said that He wanted other mothers to write stories of their secret fears and each to include a prayer—a secret prayer that is connected to their secret fear. I said, "Yes, God," and I was overtaken with joy and hope.

After taking notes on all that God had said, I prayed and waited on Him to provide me with further instructions for the book. He was quiet for a few weeks, but I had enough information to get the ball rolling. I began work on my book cover and promotional content.

Then, while walking one day at the park, I heard Him again. He said, "I am God Almighty. Nothing happens unless I allow it. If someone is to die in a plane crash, they will not die in their sleep, and if they're to die by drowning, they will not die in a car accident. Everyone dies, and I am the One who decides how and when—not the devil, not the police, not the gangs. It's me, God."

He continued to say that this book is to be used as a powerful tool to free Black mothers from the fear they have been carrying for so many centuries. It is a fear that has been slowly killing us. Like the enemy, it has come to steal, kill, and destroy our hope, peace, joy, family, and spiritual life. It's also preventing us from becoming the parents God has called us to be. "This book will set Black mothers free to live a purposeful life."

God then showed me how the children at home are affected by their mothers' fears, which are inevitably projected onto them. Fear has become the number-one threat to Black people, but we don't see it. We are blinded by it, living in a reflexive flight-or-fight mode. God wants us to breakthrough—to pull the blindfolds off and break down barriers. When we acknowledge the fear and confront it with God's Word, we can live in faith, knowing that God is in control and that we should trust the plans He has for our lives and the lives of our children.

This book is packed with real-life, raw, unfiltered stories and powerful prayers, affirmations, scriptures, holistic tools and techniques, and so much more. These stories will help our Black community to recognize that we are not alone. There are many who struggle, but there are many who have overcome. This is our legacy as a people who are strong and resilient, and we shall overcome.

Introduction

"There are few things more powerful than the faithful prayer of a righteous mother." ~Boyd K. Packer

It takes a lot of courage to share our deepest parenting worries, but worry is what we do as parents. Black mothers live in a state of deepening emotions. We feel joy each time we see our children smile, excitement watching them learn to tie their shoes, proud when they graduate each new academic level.

And we feel fear.

Black mothers carry a unique fear that the part of them that goes out separately into the world every day could meet harm. In the United States alone, violence is among the leading causes of death for Black men and boys, and racism has been linked to poor mental health outcomes. This fear is not imagined for mothers of Black children—it is a daily reality, and not just for those of us with sons but for mothers with daughters too.

As a result, Black mothers carry a larger burden, which requires them to pray a more rigorous and intentional prayer for their children's survival. Mothers with children of color pray daily that their sons and daughters come home alive. They pray, in particular, that their children do not experience race-and color-related trauma and the external fear associated with racism. Black mothers pray that their children will not be socially marginalized as they live with the fear of knowing that even though they've done everything right and necessary to raise good, law-abiding children, their offspring have become an endangered species.

This anthology highlights the depths of a mother's love, which knows no boundaries. It is in a category all by itself. A mother's love shapes cultures and molds young, impressionable individuals and provides stability and emotional availability, which is the key to their children's well-being. This powerful and inspirational anthology also brings to the forefront the secret fears that Black mothers carry deep within and how that fear controls our lives and dictates our parenting. It negatively impacts our mental, spiritual, social, and physical health, as well as our children's self-confidence, relationships, social-development, self-worth, and so much more. In addition, this fear adversely affects our relationships with our children.

As we embark on the journey to motherhood, our first stop is the birth of a child. This is no walk in the park, especially when we follow the natural process of carrying the child for nine months. Regardless of the size, shape, or color of our children, we love them as they are, and we do our best to shield them from any danger. In an equal environment where no one is treated differently, protecting and caring for our children wouldn't be such a demanding task. But this isn't the case for Black mothers.

Every Black mother teaches their children the painful lessons of why they should "behave" themselves when they are outside the home. After we successfully help our offspring navigate their childhood, adulthood comes quickly. Seeing our children grow to adults ought to bring lots of smiles; but for many of us, it brings something else—FEAR. This is because we see our fears play out on the news, including stories such as these:

- An increasing number of Blacks incarcerated in U.S. prisons for the slightest reasons
- Unfair and biased treatment in the prison system against Blacks and other minorities

These issues make us work twice as hard to ensure we give the good life to our children. We strive to provide them a world where they have a voice. Giving our children a voice helps prevent us from worrying about the following:

- Fear of our children being kidnapped or sex trafficked
- Fear of our children joining gangs or being attacked by gangs
- Fear of our children committing suicide due to ill treatment

This anthology gives us the space to address these fears and share our experiences of how fear impacted us and how we overcame. And we aren't only sharing what we were fearful of, but we also discuss how we navigated these fears and won the battle of our minds. We believe our stories resonate with other Black women. Hence, we also believe our strategies for finding victory over our fears will resonate with all Black women. The most useful weapon that we come to appreciate more and more is **prayer**.

Many do not realize the power we have available to us when we take our authority in prayer and learn how to surrender it all unto God. The truth be told, there would be no such thing as doubt, fear, or anxiety when it comes to our children because we would be on our faces before God, storming the heavenly realms in battle with the darkness and evil forces in our world for them.

The mission of this book is to bring hope, enlightenment, and meaningful cultural transformation to many mothers from our complex and intersecting stories. *The Secret Prayer of a Righteous Black Woman: The Power of a Mother's Prayer* will be a powerful resource, providing wisdom, comfort, and prayer for Black moms all over the world. The real-life, inspirational stories and powerful prayers within will bring peace, lightening the weight of unwanted burdens and worries that Black moms have been carrying since the day they learned of their conception.

The Secret Prayer of a Righteous Black Woman: The Power of a Mother's Prayer is a compilation of real stories shared by Black mothers as they hold steadily to James 5:16, which states "that the fervent prayers of the righteous are powerful!"

Ready to see our challenges and solutions?
Let's dive in.

The Perfect Revelation of the Lord
19 Psalm of David.

The heavens declare the glory of God;
And the firmament shows His handiwork.
Day unto day utters speech,
And night unto night reveals knowledge.

There is no speech nor language
Where their voice is not heard.
Their line has gone out through all the earth,
And their words to the end of the world.

In them He has set a tabernacle for the sun,
Which is like a bridegroom coming out of his chamber,
And rejoices like a strong man to run its race.
Its rising is from one end of heaven,
And its circuit to the other end;
And there is nothing hidden from its heat.

The law of the Lord is perfect, converting the soul;
The testimony of the Lord is sure, making wise the simple;
The statutes of the Lord are right, rejoicing the heart;
The commandment of the Lord is pure, enlightening the eyes;
The fear of the Lord is clean, enduring forever;
The judgments of the Lord are true and righteous altogether.

More to be desired are they than gold,
Yea, than much fine gold;
Sweeter also than honey and the honeycomb.
Moreover by them Your servant is warned,
And in keeping them there is great reward.

Who can understand his errors?
Cleanse me from secret faults.

Keep back Your servant also from presumptuous sins;
Let them not have dominion over me.
Then I shall be blameless,
And I shall be innocent of great transgression.
Let the words of my mouth and the meditation of my heart
Be acceptable in Your sight,
O Lord, my strength and my Redeemer.

> *"Have I not commanded you? Be strong and courageous. Do not be frightened, and do not be dismayed, for the Lord your God is with you wherever you go." Joshua 1:9*

Chapter 1

Moving, Changing, Living: Shifting Past Fear and Living God's Promise

by Reea Rodney

Moving, Changing, Living: Shifting Past Fear and Living God's Promise

by Reea Rodney

The United States has always fascinated me. The freedom it offers and its reward system for hard work make it an excellent place to raise a child. For an immigrant like me, the benefits are enormous and lead to a positive change in living standards. The healthcare and standard of education here are enough to live a decent life. With all these benefits, and so much more available, the States was undoubtedly where I wanted to live with my children.

When I immigrated to this country in 2006, I earned a living as a childcare provider, primarily for Caucasian families. I loved and nurtured their children like my own, and I've seen what the American environment offered them. Their needs were always met, and they didn't need to struggle. They could joke, lash out at their parents, and throw childish tantrums, and through it all, they were encouraged to be strong and independent thinkers and leaders.

My years of working as a childcare provider also showed me the downside of immigration, as it highlighted the difference between "us" and "them" and shone a light on the one thing I feared the most—racism.

Having been apart from my children for about five years, I looked forward to the day they'd join me in the United States. My children came from a place where racism didn't exist. In the Caribbean, everyone was treated equally, no matter if they were "different." My kids would be coming from an environment where children of all walks of life played together, regardless of their skin color.

After years of waiting, the day finally came. In 2012, I was full of elation when I finally saw my son and daughter. But beneath my joy was a veil of noticeable tension. That same year, Trayvon Martin, a seventeen-year-old black boy, was shot and killed by George Zimmerman. Trayvon's crime? "Walking about and looking around."

This incident scared me, and it became the boogie man beneath my bed, causing me to worry about my children's safety here—a thought that had never occurred to me before. My children were migrating from a country in which the police dispatchers did not ask for the race of a suspect. In Trayvon's case in Florida, the 911 dispatch asked for his race. A curious person might ask:

Would the emergency dispatcher provide different instructions if Trayvon hadn't been Black?
Would Trayvon be alive today if he hadn't been Black?

These thoughts made me remember how children were free to roam their neighborhoods in Trinidad with their friends, even at night. At least that's how it was in 2012. My fear of racism and violence in the United States was pervasive and seemingly unending. When my children went on simple errands, like to the corner store, I was afraid. I always instructed them to look around, being conscious of who was lurking about—even those who were supposed to protect them.

I didn't want these fearful situations for my children; I didn't want them to not be children anymore. But I gave them lessons on how the color of their skin is different and how they needed to comport themselves outside our home. Imagine soiling that childish innocence with the idea that their skin—a feature they should be proud of—makes them an easy target?

I was filled with immense anguish. The joy I felt for finally reuniting with my babies was ruined in tiny but constant drops of fear for their safety. I was sad, easily agitated, and worried. The possibility that my children, who weren't acquainted with the American environment, would experience any of this hatred was real. I was paralyzed with fear.

I felt confined in a ring, boxed in the corner, and required to fight my biggest enemy without any gloves or training.

This led me to ask myself hundreds of rhetorical questions and imagine countless "what ifs" about my children's safety. This was compounded by my lack of time with them, since I spent twelve hours working every day. I worked in the city, and I wasn't nearby if anything happened, and I desperately wanted to be. I believed that staying near them would be enough to protect them. I was always over thinking and making unnecessary and somewhat illogical inferences out of everyday situations. I was suspicious of everything.

After a while, I started to project my fears to my children. I could see how tense they felt. They sometimes got confused. I was going overboard with precautions, and I seemed to be brainwashing them to be just as afraid as me. The acclimation to their new country wasn't going as smoothly as I'd imagined, and it was all thanks to their mom, who feared a dangerous threat to her children's safety—racism.

Fear, Effects, and Changes

Mentally, I was terrified. Emotionally, I was drained. The fear of raising young Black teens (who are now young adults) in the United States was taxing my well-being. I didn't sleep well because of my heightened state of fear and countless nightmares of my son being shot and my daughter missing or in danger. I was anxious, knowing that my young son had to walk by himself to school, even though it was seven short blocks away. The thought of my daughter taking the subway to school all by herself was terrifying. But my husband and I had full-time jobs that required us to leave home at the crack of dawn, so we couldn't escort them to school.

Physically, I grew weaker. Within a couple weeks of my children's arrival in the States, I fell ill. I suffered chronic pain all over my body. It affected my mind, my happiness, my peace, and it dragged on for sixteen months. I was later diagnosed with fibromyalgia. I believe my fear played a big role because it caused me a tremendous amount of stress, which is one of the triggers of this disease.

I also became a bit paranoid about racial profiling. I instructed my sons never to wear hoodies or do-rags. I feared such outfits would cause them to be viewed as thugs or potential threats because of their skin color. Even during cold weather, I didn't allow them to wear the hoods up. And since I didn't trust them to not pull the hoods over their heads when they were not with me, I stopped purchasing them.

My position as a parent took a new subservient role. I began to cede my control to this engulfing fear, and no one knew that I was struggling in silence. I was alone.

As a child, I had lacked the support I needed to thrive and feel safe. This made me determined to give my children what I didn't have growing up. I wanted them to be confident, to feel free to express themselves with me, and to always know I'd be there for them. I wanted to give them the independence of choosing friends and members of their circles. I didn't want to dictate who they should and shouldn't be seen with. I wanted them to know they could make mature decisions and that I trusted their choices.

But with this level of debilitating fear, I was unable to fully allow them the freedom and comfort that I wanted for them. I projected my fears onto them, and while they didn't always show it, I know I made their new environment much more tense. In thinking of ways to protect them, I was hurting them and making everything worse. My parental ability was restricted, and I transferred the same limitations to my children. I took their independence away when I made them follow rules I made out of fear. I often asked my daughter, who at the time was nineteen, to let me know her location whenever she was out with friends and when she would be home, which always dampened the mood.

But one particular incident proved I had gone to the lowest depths and made me feel ashamed. When my son was seven, he had been struck by a car and lost his memory. He had to learn everything from scratch when he later came to be with me at age eleven. The doctors said it would be a miracle if he made it to college. But I believe in God, and I believe in His miracles. I disregarded their diagnosis and went to work as a mother. I motivated him. I cheered him. I cried. I prayed. I got him a tutor, and he's turned out to be one of the best people I've ever known. He's currently completing his third year in college and playing soccer, which is his dream.

At nineteen years old, during the peak of the COVID-19 pandemic in 2020, my son informed me of his plan to work construction with his cousin while on summer break. He wanted to buy a car before going back to college. Normally, a mother would be happy and proud. It's a great thing to bring up a child who is thinking ahead and willing to work for their future. I should have screamed for joy at my son's news. But I didn't. I should have been happy that my son had chosen to work hard. But I wasn't.

All for one reason—fear.

I was scared. The scene of a Black driver being riddled with bullets because he was suspected of reaching for a gun ran through my mind. When a Black American is pulled over by the cops, they think:

I'll place my hands on the steering wheel.
I won't put my hands in my pockets.
I won't make funny or hurried movements.

I couldn't bear to think of my son in that position. I was paralyzed just picturing that this young Black driver could be my son. I dreaded standing on that awful podium, with the media asking questions, becoming popular for the worst reasons on earth. I dreaded life without my child. So, I didn't want him to buy a car. I thought he was vulnerable. I thought my son being behind the wheel of a car put him close to death. I was afraid, and I secretly hoped my son did not accomplish his goal. Just three months later, he had saved the money to purchase a gently used car.

Wow! My boy had a plan and he followed it to fruition! I should have been proud, and I was. I was so proud of my son. I saw a lot of myself in him, and I thought, You raised him well. He's determined, strong, and fearless. But I also wished in that moment that he wasn't. I pretended to be happy for him, and I felt like a hypocrite. Here I was, smiling with this amazing young man I get to call my son, feeling proud of his achievement, while at the same time secretly wishing he hadn't succeeded.

That was the lowest point this fear had taken me. At that moment, this fear became my enemy number one, and I was determined to beat it.

Turning Point

I was devastated that I couldn't sincerely cheer my baby to success and that I couldn't be the pillar of strength I wanted to be for him. Many men have attained success and have attributed it to the dogged persistence of their mothers. Here my son was on a path to success, and for the very first time, I found myself watching from the sideline, terrified as he pushed toward his dreams. I wasn't coaching him. I wasn't screaming "Come on, son, you can do it!" I wasn't praying to God for his success. Oh, no! I saw myself as an invisible obstacle—all because of a debilitating fear for a situation I couldn't control.

That was the day when I said "Enough." I decided to pray as I felt something deep within my core vibrating. For some strange reason, the power of prayer became so relevant in my mind, it was if I had just discovered it for the first time. God flashed a memory of a dream that I'd had when I was pregnant with my son. In this dream, I was giving birth on a riverbank when two huge hands—God's hands—descended from heaven and picked up my son. Then I heard the voice of God, saying, "This is my son, for whom I am well pleased." God handed him back to me and said, "He's yours."

It was at that moment that I realized, this is not "my" child. I may have carried him, I may have given birth to him, but he was entrusted to my care by God. I realized that there was nothing left to do than to surrender everything to God. I had to surrender my fears. I had to surrender my doubts. And I had to rekindle the love I had for God. I also had to regain my faith in God. I fell on my knees, and that day, I cried out to my Redeemer.

I reminded God of that dream that He had given me twenty years ago. I said, "God, you gave him to me, and now I am giving him back to you. You made the way for him to get this car, you made the way for him to get his license, and now I am trusting you more than ever, to ensure that he will not become a statistic of another young Black American man shot behind the wheel of a car by the cops." I laid it all out to God as I cried. Then I let it go.

In that moment of vulnerability before God, I felt that I was delivered from my fear. It was a turning point. As the word of the Lord says in Jeremiah 29, "'For I know the plans I have for you,' declares the Lord, 'plans for welfare and not for evil, to give you a future and a hope.'" These words brought hope of the promise of a wonderful future—not just for me but for my son.

After I overcame this fear, I was inspired to defeat my fear of driving. My son and my driving instructor taught me how to drive. It's funny how our roles changed. I'm now the student, and he's the teacher.

On the day of my driving test, a real-life incident played out the fears I'd had for my son—only the outcome was different.

On January 4, 2021, my son and I had one last driving practice before my test, which was scheduled for 3:00 p.m. that day. As we were driving in our community, we were aggressively pulled over by two cop cars. In my side mirrors, I saw them rushing out from their vehicles with their guns drawn. They yelled, "Put the windows down!"

Was this really happening?

Was I experiencing the one thing I had wished to shield my son from?

I wondered these things as I sat behind the wheel, and a fear came upon me like a rushing wind. I could think of only one thing—*pray.*

And I did.

When an officer approached us, he was hostile as he demanded my driver's license. I looked over at my son, his hands held high over his head, touching the roof of the car. My heart broke because he was scared, and I was too. I gave the officer my driver's license, then I put my hands back on the steering wheel and asked what I did wrong. Everything was happening in slow motion. Then I noticed a white mist floating between the officer and myself; it looked almost like smoke.

Suddenly there was a change in the officer's tone and physical demeanor. He explained that he'd pulled us over because our window tint looked too dark, but that it was okay. He apologized for his initial tone, urged us not to be afraid, and then they drove off. As my heartbeat slowed, I reassured myself that God was in control, that He had protected us, and that He will continue to do so for my son.

It was as if God were saying, "I got you, and I got him."

I thanked God! The faith I had lost to fear started to rebuild. In times past, my heart trembled with fear. Now, it's firm. I started confronting the things that triggered my fears rather than allowing them to eat deep into me. I knocked them down one by one and reclaimed my mental space. I began clearing all thoughts from my head that my children weren't safe. Instead of visualizing all the negative things that could happen, I started calling the positive things forth.

In this state of trusting and submitting to God, His numerous blessings that I had taken for granted became clearer. I started to give gratitude for everything. If He could rescue me from the horrible fangs of COVID-19 and many other troubles I'd had, then there was nothing He couldn't do.

As a woman of faith, I know that prayer changes things, and so I purposed in my heart to see zero obstacles before me. I speak life over myself, my children, and my situations. I express gratitude to God for how far He has brought me and my family, and I reinforce my inner peace by making declarations over my life. Some of my favorites include:

- God is head over my life.
- I am superior to my fears.
- God is in control.
- I am more than enough.
- I am victorious.

Meditating and listening to my inner conversations also played key roles in helping me gain control of my overactive negative thoughts conjured by fear. I identified these negative inner conversations by connecting with my emotions, such as fear or sadness, and reframed them into positive thoughts. Now, when fear rears its ugly head, I counter it by praying, saying my affirmations, expressing gratitude, and sticking to my meditation schedule.

All these have shaped my physical, emotional, and mental well-being to function as a superior Black woman and mom. As a mother who struggled with fear when raising my Black children, I encourage you today to fear not. Proverbs 3:5–6 says, "Trust in the Lord with all of your heart and lean not to your own understanding. In all your ways acknowledge him and he will direct your path." If you experience fears like mine, try what worked for me: praying, saying affirmations, expressing gratitude, and sticking to a meditation schedule.

Prayer of Overcoming and Protection

Father God, I come before You today with thanksgiving in my heart because You are the God of yesterday, today, tomorrow, and forever. You are my merciful and loving Father, who wants the best for Your children just as I want the best for mine. Lord, I come thanking You for sparing our lives and for encamping your angels to watch over us. Lord, I thank You for Your loving kindness and Your tender mercies toward us and for Your grace, which is sufficient to keep us sound and whole.

Father, You said in Your Word that You can do exceedingly abundantly above all that I can even think or ask of You. So today, heavenly Father, I come acknowledging You for who You are in my life and in the lives of my children. You are our redeemer, You are our provider, You are our healer, You are our wall of protection, and You are our rock. We are more than conquerors through You, Christ Jesus, and because of You, all my fears and guilt are gone. Because of You, I can stand with boldness to face another day, knowing that I can do all things through You who give me strength.

In closing, Lord, I lift up every Black mom who feels like her life is spinning out of control because of fear of the unknown. I speak a calm upon her mind, body, and soul in the name of Jesus. Lord, put Your full armor upon her so that she is equipped to fight against the war in her mind. Help her to know that You didn't give her a spirit of fear, but of power, love, and a sound mind, and that the weapon formed against her mind and the minds of her children will not prosper, in Jesus's almighty name. Amen.

> *"Blessed is she who has believed that the Lord would fulfill His promises to her."* Luke 1:45

 *Chapter* **2**

Restless:
The Evanescence of Bitter Dreams

by Fenyx Blue

Restless:
The Evanescence of Bitter Dreams

by Fenyx Blue

A square house with a triangle roof under a circle sun—this is what I saw other girls drawing in elementary school. They drew their dreams, which included two kids, one dog, and a tall, dark, and handsome husband on nine by twelve-inch Manila drawing paper.

I didn't draw my dreams. My dreams and goals were too big for that paper. I never thought about how many children I would one day have or if they would have curly hair and caramel skin. I spent my twenties securing my dream job, buying my dream house, and helping other people's kids make their dreams come true. Unfortunately, in my late twenties, my doctor told me I would never be able to have any children, and pretty pictures framed in the glass of undrawn dreams that lived only in my mind began to shatter.

I had never drawn my dream children, but I had hoped for them. And when the doctor told me I could not have them, like most human beings who are denied something, this made me want them even more.

Luckily, the doctor was wrong. With prayer and favor, I did get pregnant. But then the doctor said, "You are so petite, I don't know if you will be able to carry these twins to full term." The doctor was wrong again. My fraternal twins did try to make an early exit from my womb when they were only the size of a bag of rice, but the hospital was able to stop that premature labor. Thanks to prayer and modern medicine, their early departures from my pregnancy plane without parachutes were blocked, and they both arrived on time to their destination—one at five pounds and the other five pounds and three ounces.

That was when the nightmares began. Every night, I had a recurring dream of someone stealing them, stealing her, or stealing him. In my bitter dreams, we would be at the grocery store, and someone would kidnap them. I would be securing them into their car seats, and someone would grab one of them. I even had a nightmare in which someone who held me at gunpoint asked me to choose which one would live and which one would die. After each horrible vision, I would wake up crying, frantically looking into their matching bassinets—at her in her pink onesie and him in his baby-blue one—with worry in my oval eyes. News stories of missing children flashed in my mind constantly. Amber alerts caused me ceaseless anxiety.

I kept wondering if someone would be able to sneak into our home through their bedroom windows at night. And if they were able to steal my babies, would the world care? More Black babies go missing than white babies each year. There were 800,000 reported missing Black children annually, but I rarely saw their stories on the news. The fear grew as my children grew in age. Would someone grab her and make her a sex worker? Would someone grab him to torture him for being a Black boy, born endangered? I found myself hoping my daughter did not physically develop too quickly. My daughter complained about being slim without a big booty (an asset in our community), and I silently smiled, grateful for puberty being shy and taking its time with her.

My son wondered when his height would come, and I was secretly thankful that his mature voice and stature had not arrived, only to attract fear from those who would instantly be threatened by him. Black boys don't get to become men at twenty-one. They are deemed men the moment they grow up. Once the inches start coming, they are called "little man" or "young man," even if they are only ten.

Black girls are called sexy before they are even able to learn what sex is in school. Their childhoods are stolen like precious gems by a society who rushes to deem them as adults so that they can be given adult consequences.

I peeked in on them as they slept, trying to smile when I saw him holding her tiny hand in his. I checked their windows daily. When the world saw adults, I saw the reality of two tweens who had not mastered chores, homework, or friendship yet. The person who would kidnap my son to torture him would not care that he was an honor student, had attended a Christian school, or volunteered to give birthday parties to the homeless children in our city. The person who would steal my daughter to force her to do wicked things would not see her as a child of God, a future doctor, or a little girl trying to learn lacrosse from a mom who had never even known lacrosse existed.

Yes, I was shocked, too. My baby wanted to play lacrosse. We do that, too. There are no limits to what our children can do when they are seen, but some refuse to see them as anything but something to be abused. Some see our children as property, beasts, or menaces. If my non-Black friends asked me to describe what it is like to be a Black child in America, I'd explain that childhood for Black American kids is a firecracker lit the moment you are born, held in your hands until it pops, leaving many people burned, bruised, or disfigured. It is as if the world has a fun house carnival mirror when it comes to Black children that distorts their image, and only those who love them can truly see them for who they are in this world.

Children should be able to jump in puddles, climb trees, go to the mall, and play dress up. They should receive presents—not worry, fear, or pain. But too often, this is the reality for the Black child. Instead of joy, innocence, and freedom, they quickly trade their bike rides for rides in the back of squad cars; toys for being targeted; and video games for being the victim in a real-life game, where they are never chosen to be the hero or heroine.

My sweet, brave kids wanted to leave the house, so we developed a "5 Ws and H" system. This meant they had to tell me (1) Who they were going with, (2) Where they were going, (3) Why they were going, (4) When they would return, (5) What they would be doing, and How they would let me know they were safe. I constantly volunteered to chauffeur them and their friends to the mall or school events because, armed with my taser, I hoped I could possibly protect them from potential pedophiles, sex traffickers, and kidnappers.

I don't know if you know this, but teenagers like autonomy. They didn't want a mom who calls to check on them after they walk two blocks away to a friend's house. They didn't want a mom who demands they stay on the phone until they arrive safely at their friend's home. I was that mom.

God had given me two beautiful bundles of joy. He had given me two miracles—my little girl and my little boy. So, we practiced how to scream and use profanity at the mall instead of only yelling "Help!" If someone tried to grab them so that people would pay attention. I taught my kids self-defense and how to escape the capture of someone who was larger than them.

They never left the house without charged cellphones that I could locate. I felt this was normal behavior. I felt that this is what every mother does for the safety of her child. It wasn't until I was dropping my fifteen-year-old daughter off at her boyfriend's home one day that I realized I had been paralyzed by fear. We rode past a little white boy outside playing by himself on the corner of a very busy street. He looked like he was about seven years old. He was playing in the yard by himself. I did not see a mother staring out the window watching him. I did not see a father in the yard next to him as he slid down the hill next to his house. He was smiling and free. My daughter instantly mentioned all of the things that could go wrong. She noticed everything.

"Mom, he could slide into the street. Where are his parents? Why is he out here alone? Who is watching him? How did he get so far from his house? What should we do?" I was so proud of her for asking great questions, but I was instantly sad that she couldn't just see a little boy innocently playing in his yard. Instead, she only saw danger. I don't know why I was so surprised, given that I had raised her that way. How could she see anything but danger? She and her brother had been warned of sick strangers who shop for Black children to sell, kill, or exploit. They have lived in a country where thousands of kids who look like them go missing every day without protection from authorities or timely and thorough investigations to save their lives or find them. That little white boy had probably never heard those conversations.

His mother probably didn't personally know of any missing or targeted kids. He would probably one day be fifteen years old and walking in his neighborhood to go visit his girlfriend without a parent chauffeur to make sure he made it safely. That little boy probably never had "the talk." He probably knew not to talk to strangers and to look both ways before crossing the street, but he probably had not seen little white boys set on fire or hanged. He may have even been fingerprinted or had dental photos taken for his records, but were his parents waiting every day for a call that would require them to need these things?

This was my reality. It was the reality of many parents that I knew. The friends of my twins also have protective mothers who watch over them like lionesses protecting their cubs. We have a tight-knit tribe, so our kids always have eyes on them. Our dream for our kids is not to be fearful, but to be faithful. When I listened to my daughter, I heard fear in her voice. I sensed trepidation—trepidation that could curse every generation of my family. I declared generational blessings and not curses over my family, but to be honest, I was still afraid.

Have you ever tried to pray with fake strength, but you are full of doubt?

I dropped her off, knowing she would be okay, but still worried about all of the potential problems that could happen on her date. She had told me who, what, when, where, why, and how, but every Black mom knows that you are never secure until your child is back in your sight. I was not walking by faith, but I was certainly walking by sight.

In order to decrease my own fears, I went to my mother to confess that I was still having nightmares about someone stealing my children. She listened to me while nodding at all of the right places, as experienced mothers do. When I finished speaking, she held my hand and asked me who I believe loves my children more—"you or God?" It was an unexpected response because my mother normally gives great advice. She usually shares amazing stories and anecdotes. She rarely responds with a question.

I paused to think, though of course I knew the answer was God. God was the reason they even existed when science had confirmed they should not have been born. God was the reason my daughter even had a name, since He had whispered it to my spirit as I'd prayed for one. (I named my daughter Legacy.) God was the reason that my son, who was breech and the reason I had to have a C-section, came only two minutes later than his "older" sister and was healthy and happy.

The answer to my mother's question was most certainly God. "God loves them more, Mom," I said, knowing she was setting me up but not knowing how to evade her direct question.

"So why are you worried about protecting them? You're my child. He protects you for me. Doesn't he?" She asked two questions this time, but I could barely answer one before I began to weep.

It is always okay to cry in front of a mother who loves you more than anything in this world, so I let the tears fall unapologetically. She was absolutely correct. I had been so worried that I would not be able to protect my twins from predators twenty-four hours a day. I had forgotten that the wise say, if you are going to pray, don't worry, and if you are going to worry, don't pray. Each night I was praying over them. Yet, I wasn't trusting that God would protect them as they slept or every moment that they were awake.

I could not sleep at night because I was not allowing God to keep my two "dreams" alive and well.

Her words reminded me of Matthew 6:25–34, which states, "Therefore I tell you, do not be anxious about your life, what you will eat or what you will drink, nor about your body, what you will put on. Is not life more than food, and the body more than clothing? Look at the birds of the air: they neither sow nor reap nor gather into barns, and yet your heavenly Father feeds them. Are you not of more value than they? And which of you by being anxious can add a single hour to his span of life? And why are you anxious about clothing? Consider the lilies of the field, how they grow: they neither toil nor spin, yet I tell you, even Solomon in all his glory was not arrayed like one of these." This scripture reminded me that I did not have to work or worry because God already knows what I need and has already planned to take care of those needs for those He loves.

Her words were a reminder that I could focus on being a mom instead of a security guard or a god to my children. God was more than capable of being their shield from the evil ones who come to kill, steal, or destroy.

I decided not to focus on the negative, but to instead begin to manifest the positive desires and dreams that I have for my children. I began to go to bed hopeful of the woman and man my children would become. I began to envision in my future blessed grandchildren. I saw my children happy, safe, and protected from all hurt, harm, and danger. This future began to show up in my dreams. I began to have dreams with my son laughing. I woke up with echoes of his giggles in my heart.

All those years I had wasted focusing on stealing instead of on the gift of love that had been given by God. All of those years I had spent thinking someone would kidnap my children, forgetting who gave them to me in the first place. I began to choose to remember that God is the best sleeping pill because, with Him by your side, we moms can finally rest knowing that our dreams are safely tucked in His omnipotent, omniscient, omnipresent hands. Each night, I can fall to my knees in my square house with the triangle roof under the circle moon, knowing that I am in good shape because the Father up above protects all mothers and their children.

A Prayer for Peace of Mind

Father God,

This mother thanks You for Your protection. I can rest knowing I am loved by the best. I am grateful for Your being a shield for me and my children. Your Word says You never leave nor forsake us. This means I can close my eyes and trust that You are always near. This means that You are with my children even when I am not. I do not need to be afraid because You promise to rescue me from every evil attack. You are my hiding place. The enemy cannot attack what he cannot see. You cover me. Thank You for gifting me with strength and courage. Thank You for reminding me that no weapon forged against me (or my babies) will prevail (Isaiah 54:17). You said that those who oppose me will be as nothing and perish (Isaiah 41:11). You say that I can stand against the devil's schemes because of Your power.

You say that the same power that is in You dwells in me. You say that I am created in Your image. Thank You for loving me. Thank You for creating me. Thank You for empowering me and trusting me to watch over my children, who are Your children. I know that You love them. You protect those You love. You sacrifice for those You love. You gave your only child for those You loved. Thank You for being the best example of parenthood. I promise to put on the full armor of God and to follow Your lead, knowing You are always on watch. I know that with You by my side I can walk through fire and not be burned (Isaiah 43:2).

I will not allow the enemy to kidnap my dreams or to steal the destiny of my children. I will not permit anxiety to outrank my faith in You. Today, I kill stress and bury it in a grave next to my fears. Today, I promise to let my light so shine before men so that they may see Your good works and glorify my Father which is in heaven (Matthew 5:16). Today, I promise to dream big dreams like Solomon and Joseph, knowing that no one can take away the dreams that You make. Thank You for making me a mother. Thank You for a good night's sleep with sweet dreams. In the mighty, perfect name of Jesus Christ, I pray and say, amen.

Fear not, for I am with you; be not dismayed, for I am your God; I will strengthen you, I will help you, I will uphold you with my righteous right hand. Isaiah 41:10

Chapter 3

Out of the Depths of Darkness: A Mother's Journey to Salvation

by Rhonda Small Peters

Out of the Depths of Darkness: A Mother's Journey to Salvation

by Rhonda Small Peters

*W*illiam Shakespeare got it right when he said "death is a fearful thing."

We are none of us strangers to death; indeed death is a part of life. We all harbor fears of falling victim to it or losing someone we love to it. I have not only thought about dying, but I've stared death in the face. I've long made peace with the thought of dying, but I've never been able to master the acceptance of losing someone I love. To suffer the loss of a family member or lifelong friend is to become acquainted with sorrow. But to lose a child is heartbreak in its purest form—every parent's worst nightmare.

When I became a parent, death became my most formidable foe. I looked at my kids and I couldn't imagine a world where they no longer existed. My fears about death rekindled. Is this fear unique to me? No, I believe the fear of losing a child prematurely to the claws of death is a hidden fear carried by all parents. When the biblical character Job heard the news of the death of his children alongside the other calamities that had befallen him, he declared, "That which I have feared the most has come upon me." His greatest fears had become his reality.

There is no doubt in my mind that God never intended that a parent should ever have to bury a child. Yet it is a grim reality that many have had to face this terrible ordeal. The loss of a loved one can be traumatic, but when it's a parent bewailing the loss of a child, their pain can be so raw that it leaves an indelible imprint.

It's instinctive to want to protect your child. Sadly, there will always be things beyond our control—the unforeseen accident or that unexpected illness. Against these things you cannot guard, and if such a hand is dealt to you, you can only hope to console yourself by saying "it is the will of God." On the other hand, it's quite a different matter to have the life of your child snuffed out at the hands of a monster, senselessly murdered by someone who didn't consider the hurt and pain that such a cruel act would bring. It can only be asked: "Is there any balm that can soothe such a wound?"

Truth be told, while there is nothing as life-changing and fulfilling as being a parent, it can be a worrisome responsibility. When your kids are small, you watch over them as a hen shelters her chicks beneath the cover of her wings, courageously shielding them from predators. However, inevitably, there comes a time when they begin to venture out on their own, and although you are keenly aware that there is always danger lurking in the shadows, you try to lay aside your anxieties.

It doesn't help that the young tend to be carefree and adventurous—reminiscent of a toddler, driven by natural curiosity, who is intent on exploring every nook and cranny, blissfully unaware that even in his familiar terrain there may lie danger. In the young adult's bid to lay claim to their independence, they can also be obstinate and stubborn, which in itself adds another element of concern. They demand the freedom to select their own career paths, choose their friends, and navigate their own way, and you have no choice but to relax the vice-like grip maintained throughout their childhood.

Shamelessly, we may sometimes employ a subtle form of manipulation, sharing our fears with our kids in the hope that they would be a little more wary. But it is the folly of youth that they feel almost invincible, thinking to themselves, "That can never happen to me." Sadly, our pleas fall on deaf ears. As a parent you open your heart to your kids, giving them a glimpse into your world, but predictably they make light of your fears: "Mom, you're being paranoid," or "Don't worry, I've got this," or worse yet, "Why are you trying to stop me from living my life? You've lived yours." They don't understand, and you can relate because you once stood in their shoes.

Grudgingly, you've had to accept that as much as you may wish otherwise, you cannot protect them from the ugliness of the world, or even from themselves.

So, you adapt and attempt to manage your fear by keeping it buried; but truthfully, it's never far from the surface. It remains there unless unearthed by a news headline or a traumatic experience. I discovered this firsthand when my son's father was murdered, and I witnessed his mother's agony as she looked at his badly decomposed body lying on the ground. It traumatized me, cutting into my very soul. But no one looking at me could tell, because even in the face of my growing fear, I presented a stoic facade. Long after, I hadn't spoken of that day or the terror it invoked within me, for fear that speaking of it would give my fears life. I did not want to tempt fate. However, with the passage of time, a nagging fear morphed into an oppressive fear.

I have no doubt that there are others like myself who have been touched by violence and left to labor under the weight of trauma-induced fear. My fears revolved around my kids—the uncertainty of tomorrow. For a parent who is afraid to lose their child to a world where crime and violence is running rampant, the fear of the unknown coupled with the fear of loss can become consuming. I lived this reality for years.

If I have gained any wisdom from my experience, it is the knowledge that fear left unchecked has the power to become crippling—not only to you but also to those within your orbit. Fears are not to be fed but starved. Regardless of what your fears may be, there are practical ways that you can marshal and conquer them. Believe me when I say that you can regain your peace of mind. But to do so, you will have to confront your demons. You have to deal with all unresolved baggage that can trigger emotional responses. If you are to successfully free your mind from constricting fear, it's imperative that you put the axe to the root of your fears.

For me, this meant I had to deal with the mental, emotional, and psychological aftereffects brought about by the hopelessness and loss I felt when I saw my son's dad—his mutilated and partially burnt body was abandoned in the bushes. Like garbage tossed to the side of the road.

My son's dad had been kidnapped, and as the days passed and no ransom request was received, our hope began to wane, and we feared that he was dead. I can still vividly remember receiving the news that his body had been found—my worst nightmare had become my reality. His abductors had murdered him. I could not escape the torrent of feelings that arose like a gale storm within me. Emotionally, I went inside of myself in an effort to disconnect from my emotions. I struggled internally, refusing to be sucked into the vortex of grief that beckoned me, rationalizing that to do so would make no difference; the hands of time could not be turned back. He was gone. I had to be strong for my son.

At first, I was resolutely determined that I would not go to see his body. But then, I began to feel as though he was calling me to his side. I was being drawn by an almost imperceptible but irresistible magnetic pull that weakened my resolve until, almost involuntarily, I found myself making the trek through the bushes to get to where his body had been found. With every step, my heart filled with dread. I didn't know if I was prepared for what I would see or for how it would impact me. Whenever I close my eyes and carry my mind back to that day, the thing I remember most is the smell. His body had already begun to decompose, and though the air was foul, it struck me that I almost didn't mind it, because it was him. That was his scent, and it was the closest that I would ever get to him again.

His mom was kneeling by his body; she was shrieking and wailing as she bemoaned the loss of her son. As I drew nearer, our eyes connected. I saw the despair reflected in her eyes, and her cries seemed to grow louder. I have always felt that at that moment she hadn't been seeing me, but her grandson, and it intensified her pain. As the scene of her grief unfolded before my eyes, a chill traveled through my body, causing my heart to freeze. This became a defining moment for me.

I thought about my sons. Lord knows I didn't want such a horrible end for any of them—their lives prematurely snuffed out by violence. "Please, God, don't ever let this be my portion." Even as she continued to mourn over her son, I silently wailed for mine. How could he cope with the loss of his father in such a violent way? As I walked away, I was certain of one thing: life, for me, would never be the same.

Even though I had always harbored fears of losing my children, what I had witnessed caused my normal, rational fears to juxtapose into a sort of paranoia. I became so overburdened with the fear that one of my kids could be murdered that I could not give myself over fully to parenting them with joy. I couldn't live in the moment. Instead, I lived in fearful anticipation of the future—when they would begin to live their own lives, and I would lose whatever parental control I had that made it possible for me to keep them safe.

Make no mistake about it, fear, whether real or imagined, has the power to hold you hostage, carrying you to some dark and morbid places. I found myself praying every moment that they were not in my eyesight and would only feel peace when they were under my watchful gaze. I felt as though the spirit of untimely death hovered around every corner, waiting to snatch one of them from my hands. I became mentally exhausted, spiritually weakened, and emotionally drained. I couldn't continue carrying this burden, but I couldn't find my way through the maze.

As a single parent of five boys, I felt this increased the probability of losing one of them to violence. The fact that they were all individuals, with differing views and perspectives, only served to increase my fears, which threatened to choke the life out of me. I found myself grappling daily with the fear that any one of my sons could somehow fall in with the wrong crowd and be negatively influenced, or be in the wrong place at the wrong time, or be involved in a confrontation that would cost them their life. And although my fears revolved around that of losing my kids, it was my eldest son who troubled my spirit the most.

I wondered if his fate could somehow be intertwined with his father's, leading him to suffer a similar destiny.

His father's murderer has never been found, and the mystery surrounding his death fueled my fears. I also knew that suffering the violent loss of a parent could stir emotions in a young man that if not confronted could easily give rise to bitterness, hatred, and anger. I saw depression skulking around him, and fears of developing suicidal tendencies also flitted through my mind. I knew that there wasn't a violent bone in his body, but I was always on high alert because I felt that his unresolved grief could one day erupt, creating a maelstrom of misery.

As to be expected, I became overly protective, trying to do the impossible. To my boys, it felt like overkill because they couldn't see what I was seeing. I was battling against unknown realities that had not yet presented themselves, but that didn't make them any less real to me. I imagined drive-by shootings, stray bullets, fatal fights, and more. I knew that my fears had the power to be transmitted to them, sending signals that would impact them negatively, making them fearful or inviting rebellion.

I hadn't opened up to anyone about my fears. Not because I feared being misunderstood—I knew that the fear of losing a child is a fear that every parent carries by default—but because it would mean talking about my unresolved feelings over the murder of my son's father.

In hindsight, I don't think my fear was misplaced, but it was definitely exaggerated. It's a documented fact that premature death by homicide and suicide is higher in young Black men in comparison to young men of any other ethnicity. As such, I felt as though the odds were already against my sons. For a young Black male, the likelihood of losing his life to violence can be exceedingly greater—not because death is a respecter of persons but because of the negative influence and exposure to elements such as drugs, gangs, poverty, racialism, and victimization, which are much more prevalent in Black communities.

Although my boys were each exposed to the same basic influences, the death of my first son's father seemed to make him a prime candidate in my eyes to become a statistic. My fears came to a head when it was time for him to leave the nest. He was about to attend university, and as his departure drew near, I found myself struggling with intense separation anxiety. Even though he had received counselling, I still didn't believe that he had ever fully come to terms with, not only the death of his father, but the fact that justice had never been served. I wondered how this would shape his outlook of the world and his ability to interact with others in the face of trying circumstances. I was afraid that something negative could happen, serving as a trigger, and I would not be there to help him manage it.

The university environment, to my worried mind, opened the door to all the things that I feared the most—a dystopian world offering everything that could cause a young man to spiral out of control. Though I was proud of him and ecstatic that my firstborn was about to transcend even my own scholastic achievements, I couldn't give myself over to fully celebrating his accomplishments. My imagination was running wild, and I could not contain it; the fear that I could lose my son to homicidal violence had me in its grip, and it had almost eaten me alive.

And one day, when I was at my wits' end, I cried out to God, asking Him to "please deliver me from my fears." Suddenly, an unfamiliar song dropped into my spirit. I didn't know the words, but I was humming, all the while trying to catch the song. And then, just like that, the words began to form in my mind, and I realized the song was "God Sent His Son." I grabbed my hymnal and looked it up, and my eyes lit on the second verse:

> *How sweet to hold a newborn baby,*
> *And feel the pride and joy he gives.*
> *But greater still the calm assurance,*
> *This child can face uncertain days because He lives.*
> *Because He lives, I can face tomorrow.*
> *Because He lives, all fear is gone.*
> *Because I know He holds the future,*
> *And life is worth the living just because He lives.*

As I read the words, I realized that God was reassuring me through this song—my eldest son and all of my other kids would be okay.

I had to let my son go. I wouldn't be there with him in this new phase of his life, but he would be in the company of someone much better able to keep him safe and protected than I. God would have his back. I felt something being released from me spiritually; my body seemed to relax, and the fear left me.

Fear is primarily a natural instinct that forewarns of impending danger—like a blinking neon sign that grabs your attention—intended by God to safeguard not only our bodies but also our souls. However, a *spirit* of fear is another matter completely. This spirit preys on your peace of mind and locks you into a mental prison, enslaving and robbing you of your ability to reason and see your way through the confusion.

Regardless of what your fears may be, deliverance will only be materialized when your efforts are holistic, capturing mind, body, and soul. At the height of my fears, I could define what I was going through. I had practical head knowledge that could have given me momentary relief; but my complete victory came when I realized that my battle was not merely physical but also spiritual. I was in bondage to this fear, and I needed to be set free. I couldn't do it on my own.

Our heavenly Father has not given us a spirit of fear, but of love and of power and of a sound mind. He does not want us to be bogged down by fears but confident in our assurance that His perfect love for us is able to cast out all fear.

In my darkest moment, when I felt as though I was sinking into the quicksand of despair, God stretched out His hand and pulled me from its depths. I was no longer a slave to fear.

I am free!

A Prayer Against the Spirit of Fear

Heavenly Father, omnipotent God, creator and protector to all: I magnify and exalt Your name. Lord, as a parent, fears for my children's safety sometimes threaten to overwhelm me. I pray that my heart shall not faint but wax strong and that my faith and courage shall not waver but shall be indomitable in the face of every fear in the mighty name of Jesus. I stand on Your Word that urges me to not be afraid but to know that You are with me and will strengthen me and uphold me with Your right hand of righteousness. Your perfect love emboldens me that I am able to bind and cast out every spirit of fear in the mighty name of Jesus. I reject every lie that would hold me hostage to fear.

Lord, I'm thankful that You have not given me a spirit of fear but of power and of love and of a sound mind. I arrest every fear and the spirit of fear in the mighty name of Jesus. I lift my children before You, and as You have entrusted them into my care even now I commit them into Your hands. I trust You to shield them from every fiery dart of the enemy, that no weapon formed against them shall prosper in the mighty name of Jesus. I hold on to Your Word that promises that the seed of the righteous shall be delivered, confident that regardless of what the future may hold, my children shall remain sheltered beneath the cover of Your wings.

Amen.

> *But now, this is what the LORD says— he who created you, Jacob, he who formed you, Israel: "Do not fear, for I have redeemed you; I have summoned you by name; you are mine. Isaiah 43:1*

Chapter 4

Jail Is Hell:
The Fear and Action to Keep My Sons Free from the Criminal Justice System

by Michelle W. Fuqua

Jail Is Hell:
The Fear and Action to Keep My Sons Free from the Criminal Justice System

by Michelle W. Fuqua

I am the proud mother of two young adult Black men. There is not a time when I am not concerned about their well-being and safety. During their childhood, I strove to keep them safe from so many threats and dangers.

Interaction with the criminal justice system—even at the ground level when dealing with the police—conveys danger and represents a place of fear for me. I have tried to overcome my fear and negative attitudes about the criminal justice system; however, recent events in our country awoke the gorilla of hypervigilance that I keep under lock and key.

Many years ago, when my sons were early elementary age, we stopped at a gas station while vacationing. We went inside to purchase some refreshments. My oldest boy got away from me for a minute on the candy aisle. When we returned to the car, I noticed that he had something in his hand. He had brought candy out of the store that we did not purchase. Had he meant to steal the candy? I do not think so. He had not put any thought into his actions. He'd seen something he wanted, and maybe he'd intended to bring it to me. I do not know. I do know that there was no reason for him to steal the candy because I would buy them anything they wanted. There was not a concern or issue that would have caused him to steal the candy.

I recognized the outcomes that a situation like this could have for him as a Black child. Some store clerks would get nasty (we experienced this often), perhaps call the police. Others might allow him the opportunity to correct his mistakes. You never know how someone is going to respond. He was just a kid, but at that moment, I saw his future unfold before me. It terrorized me because a harmless situation such as this could spiral out of control. Maybe not at the tender age of five or six. But throughout his teenage years and young adult life, small decisions he might make, thinking they're not a big deal, could turn into deal-breakers. These decisions could lead to encounters with the police that result in arrests.

I always had the irrational but understandable hope that if one of my boys got arrested, he would make it to jail in one piece. There is almost a sick rejoicing to know that he is safe in a jail cell. I also feared the long-term devastation that these incidents could have on their future. A criminal record would limit their opportunities.

This scenario played out in my head so quickly as we sat there in the car. I do not think five minutes had passed, and this fully developed future burst forth in full color.

I treated this as a severe transgression, and I might have overreacted. I often overreacted about such things. I asked him, "Did you steal the candy?"

He was looking at me with his eyes stretched wide. I took his hand and informed him, "We are taking the candy back inside because you cannot have the candy if we do not pay for it."

I took him back inside, and we paid for the candy. I let him keep it. I wanted to make this a teachable moment without too much drama and stress. I was not going to demoralize him. He was young and did not understand all the ramifications, but I explained to him about the culture.

I told him, "You are a little Black boy, and you will grow into a fine young Black man. But there are people in certain situations in your environment that could cause you harm. Because of that, you must always be diligent. Always think about what you are doing. You need to make good decisions because you will not get a do-over!"

He looked at me, and I knew that he did not understand everything I was saying. I said it anyway.

As we drove away from that gas station, I thought back to when I was a young girl. I had moments in my teenage years when I was a terror. I had a group of friends who were trouble waiting to happen. One evening, when I was twelve or thirteen years old, police officers pursued me and my friends. We ran because that is what you do—you run! We hid in a field behind a house until late in the evening. We were more afraid of the police catching us and taking us to our parents! All we were doing was trying to have some fun in a quiet town. You would have thought we'd robbed a bank, but our infraction was minor. The weight of that offense compared to the effort spent attempting to apprehend us was incomparable. This event set the framework for how I viewed my sons' chances. It drove my fear for my sons. I wondered if my sons in such a situation would receive mercy.

I want to talk to you about my fear. It is a gnawing anxiety that runs deep. I was fearful of any interaction between the police and my two Black sons and their friends, who spent so much time at my house. I was blessed to feel as if I had more than two boys. Many of these boys I met through Christian activities. Our faith was central to all our social interactions.

One of my core scriptures is Luke 4:18, in which Jesus says, "The Spirit of the Lord is upon me, ... He has sent me to proclaim freedom for the prisoners." Freedom is a concept that deals with liberty, justice, the pursuit of happiness, self-actualization, and the ability to dwell in peace and safety. These concepts are dear to my heart. They are something that I believe are covenant rights and benefits that we possess. Jesus encouraged the masses to find rest in Him because His burden is easy, and His yoke is light. His offer represents the freedom of the Christian life. I realize that my fear deprived us of our liberty. My only objective at the time was to steer my boys through to adulthood safely and without any police encounters.

I had witnessed the disdain and disrespect that some officers display toward Black Americans. My childhood environment was one in which I experienced police officers coming into the home. They were rude. Did they treat others experiencing similar domestic issues with the same disdain? The experience created innate stress and fear. It is a hovering fear, and raising sons put it into overdrive. It ran off a cliff after the gas station incident!

I sometimes think that because my sons attended predominantly white Christian schools, they did not believe in the real danger I attempted to protect them from. I needed them to recognize that some people did not automatically see a nice young man, a well-mannered Christian boy, when they looked at them. They saw a Black boy. Indeed, their history classes and some of the other assumptions led them to believe a false narrative. I constantly corrected the history so that they would understand that they would be treated differently. *Yes, you attend a good school, but some people see the color of your skin first. These same people are threatened by your existence and will call the police on you. When the police show up, they will not give you the benefit of the doubt.*

The business of crime and incarceration created an imperative to lock up my sons for the smallest of infractions. After all, the perception was that they have an inherent capacity for criminality, violence, thieving, etcetera. The system was slanted against them, and if they got in the system, I knew that there was nothing that I could do about it.

My number one goal was to keep my sons from negative interactions with the criminal justice system. I talked to them about it all the time.

I tried to make them understand the society in which they lived.

"You live in a country that is free, in which you can accomplish anything that you decide to do. You have an advantage because you have more resources than your father and I had. You have more resources than a lot of other people in your age group. You have opportunities to be and do anything that you can dream of."

This was juxtaposed with the following:
"Expect people to be afraid of you. Because of their inherent bias, they see you as a threat."

This is interesting because when you look back over history, Black people are the ones who ought to be afraid. And we are, in a lot of cases, but not to the point where it is a paralyzing kind of fear. It is more of a watchful hesitation, in which we wait for the moment we must respond to something bad that has happened.

I told them, "When you go out in public, remember all that I have taught you regarding how to behave. Carry yourself as one with respect and dignity. Respect your elders. Don't let anyone lead you to do anything wrong.

"If you get pulled over by a police officer, do not get out of the car. Roll your window down, and put your hands on the steering wheel. Wait until the officer asks for your driver's license and registration, then slowly retrieve them so it doesn't look like you're reaching for a weapon. Pick up the phone and call us and put it on speaker phone so we can hear the entire conversation."

"Do not be alone in certain neighborhoods after dark."

"Be careful hanging out in large groups. Y'all Black boys together are seen as a gang."

"Do not do anything to fit the profile. No hoodies. No, you cannot have a tattoo or a nose ring!"

These are the things that I shared with my sons.

There are other actions that I took to keep them safe. I controlled their social world as much as possible. When they were younger, I was extremely strict about who they could hang out with, when they could hang out with them, and where they could go. As they grew older and wanted to hang out with their friends, I fretted over the silly things boys sometimes do to end up in trouble.

I allowed them the freedom to hang out with their friends because, as they grew into young men, they had to have some wisdom, some seasoning in public without parental oversight. They needed to grow and learn how to carry themselves. I could not keep them locked up in the house. I could not hide them to protect them from what was in the world.

There were many times when I witnessed other people's children getting in trouble and getting locked up. Their treatment was often disproportionate to the crime. Sentencing was often severe. I did not want that to happen to my sons. I did not want them to run with people who were disruptive or troublemakers. Fortunately, they made friends from the circle that we drew around their young lives. Some would say that this left them naive in some ways.

I want you to know that over time I had to release all fear. I grew in my faith and embraced peace. That does not mean that things changed; rather I changed how I processed the threat. It is easy to tell someone to release fear. But what does that mean? It means that we cannot let fear dictate our actions.

Courage does not happen in a vacuum. Courage is only courage if you understand fear. Set some daily goals for how you will manage your fear and anxiety. Find productive activities for yourself and your children. I live by my affirmations. Be patient because it can take some time to work free from fear.

I recognize that God has not given me the spirit of fear but of power, love, and a sound mind. I realize that we are responsible for strategically raising our children in the direction that we would have them go. All the decisions that I made in their lives were made to keep them safe. We attempted to provide an avenue in which they could prosper as young men.

I did not always get it right. I look back now and see many things that I would change if I had the opportunity to do them over. You can never predict the repercussions of the decisions that you make. All you can do is your absolute best for your sons. I involved them in groups with like-minded people. We had a community bubble for our children that we nurtured and protected to the best of our abilities.

The sad thing is that now they are grown, and the dangers that exist in our society are real and sinister. Cell phones and social media are turning everyone into a reporter. The masses can see what was previously hidden. My sons are free to live their lives as they desire. They now choose their friends from groups that I have no control over. The only choice I have now is to release them into the hands of God and pray for them.

The fear of incarceration was tied to the fear of police brutality. I hoped that if the police pulled over one of my sons, he would get to go to jail instead of riding in an ambulance. I took the time to have multiple conversations with my sons. *If you don't watch yourself, if you don't behave, if you're not paying attention to your surroundings and thinking through your actions, you will end up in jail, and jail is hell.* "So, it's jail, then hell." This was a phrase that we used to say in my house.

My goal was to ensure that they did not have to live that out. With the mindset that I have today, I recognize that there were some better affirmations, truths from the Word of God that produced a positive attitude. We prayed, studied, and learned scripture. In retrospect, I would share the facts about our society with them, but I would also equip them with the mindset of a champion. I would help them develop the perspective of someone who understands their value and their place in society and is willing to take a stand on their behalf.

If you are raising sons, I understand all the fears that you will encounter through the years. I want to encourage you to remember that she who dwells in the secret place of the Most High shall abide under the shadow of the Almighty. We wrestle not against flesh and blood but against principalities, powers, dominions, and rulers of darkness in high places. Therefore, our first line of defense in overcoming natural opposition is to pray like a warrior. If you are not a Christian or you do not pray, develop affirmations that you can say that will help to align yourself with universal truth.

Secondly, I think that choosing the environment that my children were exposed to was a good strategy. I wish I'd had more choices. I would have preferred greater diversity in their schools. Still, choose your environments and choose the people with whom you are going to socialize. Vet the families in your circle. Make sure that you all have a common expectation for behavior and discipline. Finally, be free to pursue your goals and your dreams for your sons. Live the freedom and experience the liberty that is yours and your sons' in Christ Jesus and available in concept and reality in the United States of America.

A Prayer of Covering

Dear Lord God, I give you all the glory, honor, and praise. You are all-powerful, all-knowing, ever-present. That is in our favor because there is no place that our sons can go where You are not there with them. If they descend into the pits of hell, You are there with them. You said You would never leave us nor forsake us. We stand on that truth.

No weapon formed against our sons will prosper. Danger may come on every side, and they are protected from it all. You saved our sons. You sent Your Son, Jesus Christ, that whoever believes in Him would not perish but have everlasting life. You placed a standard around our sons that the enemy cannot get through. I thank You because they are so hidden in Christ that no one can find them to hurt, harm, or endanger them.

God, I come against every demonic plan, every device, every scheme against their success in life. I cancel it out in the name of Jesus. Their minds are anointed, Lord, that they can see and think according to Your Word. They are respectful because that is how we raised them. They are resourceful. They shall grow into mighty men of honor and courage. They shall live their lives in a way that glorifies You. Lord, I pray this in Your Son, Jesus Christ's, mighty name. Amen.

> *As one whom his mother comforts, so I will comfort you; you shall be comforted in Jerusalem. Isaiah 66:13*

Chapter 5

Reaction:
A Mother's Fear of History Repeating Itself

by Debra Turner-Ray

Reaction:
A Mother's Fear of History Repeating Itself

by Debra Turner-Ray

*S*tatistics say that one in every four Black American girls/ women will be sexually abused before the age of eighteen. One in every nine girls and one in every fifty-three boys under the age of eighteen experience sexual abuse or assault at the hands of an adult. Every sixty-eight seconds, an American is sexually assaulted, and every nine minutes that victim is a child.

Every mother worries about this type of thing happening to their child. When our children are not in our eyesight, anything can happen. Molestation can happen anywhere—at home, a friend's house, school, or even church. As a Black American mom, I had this fear for my children when they were away from home. Fear can consume you, and you lose trust in people. I did at an early age.

Here's My Story

"Debbie, you have to stay home from school tomorrow because the telephone man is coming to install an extra phone line."

"That's great, but I don't want to be at home by myself. I'm only twelve—who will be here with me?"

"Your brother can stay with you if you're that scared."

"Mama, he's four! How can he protect me?"

"Well, your dad and I have to work, and one day out of school will not hurt. You will be just fine. They will be here between nine and twelve, so clean up and be dressed."

When the doorbell rang, it scared me because I had fallen asleep after my parents left for work. Needless to say, in typical Debbie fashion, I had not cleaned up, and I still had on my pajamas when the phone man came. He was a young Caucasian male, about twenty to twenty-one years old; he was about five feet, seven inches, with dirty blond hair.

I showed him where to put the new phone, and I went and sat on my bed with my brother. Fear swept over me because the man kept looking at me strangely. It seemed as though I had been sitting in my room for a long time, but in reality, it had only been a few minutes. I guess I wanted him to hurry up and go because my mom had a tendency to come home from work early, and with the house not being clean and me not being dressed, I would get a whipping.

Then, all of a sudden, the man started winking at me. That was so creepy. I wanted to use the bathroom, but I was afraid to move off the bed. My little brother was just as happy as ever, without a care in the world, and here I was scared to death. I was afraid to move because the man was watching me very closely. Being a child, I can honestly say this was a new fear.

When he finished the job, he came into my room and sat down next to me. My heart was beating so fast I thought it was going to jump out of my chest. He put his hand on the small of my back and started rubbing in a circular motion. This was so uncomfortable, but I didn't know what to do. I was only twelve.

Then he said, "How does that feel?"

I said, "I guess it's okay."

He said, "Maybe you would like it if I tried some other things."

I said, "No, I don't think so, sir."

"Oh, I'm not that old—you don't have to call me sir."

"Okay, well, my brother doesn't like seeing people bother his sister."

"Well, we will take care of that. Hey, lil' buddy, you want to see my big telephone truck?"

My brother started jumping up and down and screaming, "YES, YES, YES!"

"Okay, go look out the front window."

That boy ran so fast you would have thought lightning had struck him. The only thought that came to my mind was *I'm going to kill him later—before mama gets home.*

After my brother left the room, this man got down on his knees and started rubbing my legs up and down. Then he asked, "Do you like that?"

I said, "I don't think so. I don't know—nobody has ever done that to me before."

"Well, if no one has ever done that, then maybe you'll like this." Just as he was getting ready to go under my nightgown, my brother came flying back in the room, and I scooped him up and sat him on my lap. The phone rang, and it was my mom wondering if the man had finished. I told her he was getting ready to go.

He went and packed up his things and left. I watched out the window to make sure he was gone. What a relief that was over. In all my twelve years, I'd never been that scared. I did tell my parents what happened; of course, I omitted that I still had on my pajamas. In my mind, I always wondered if I didn't have on my pajamas, would he still have touched me like that?

*   *   *

As a Black American single mother of two—one son and one daughter—fear is a normal part of life. This is mentally draining because you want to keep your children close. Children don't understand when you tell them they can't spend the night at a friend's house. They think you're being mean, but in reality, you are keeping them safe. Just because it happened to you as a child, you don't want it to happen to your kids. The scars on the inside don't heal as fast as the outside wounds. Emotionally, this takes a toll because you don't trust anyone around your children. This will literally drive you crazy because you are always on high alert. Because of what happened to me as a child I was overly protective, especially when they wanted to go play with children I did not know.

They were never allowed to go inside people's houses to play. Spiritually, I was torn because I knew about God, and I knew He existed; but where was He when I was a kid? Concealing your fear from children is very challenging because they always want to know, "Why can't I go over to my friend's house?" Emotionally, this is taxing because you can't scream at them because of your past, so you keep a cool head and say, "Because I said so, and I'm your mother." Sometimes this works and sometimes not, but it's worth a try just to maintain some control and your sanity.

When it came to parenting, I was just as on edge with my son as I was with my daughter. Both of my children were popular, so before they went anywhere, I had to meet the parents and get phone numbers. They used to say, "My mama be trippin'." But it didn't matter; I was just being a mama. They didn't know how bad that experience bothered me.

Whenever they would go somewhere and come home, I'd ask if anyone had touched them in their private area. They always said no. I'm grateful, but that made them curious enough to ask me why I always asked those kinds of questions. I always said, "I'm just asking," because I wasn't ready to reveal that part of my life to them until they became older. They understood when they became parents themselves.

One thing I did differently from my parents was that I never left my children home alone when any service workers were coming to repair something. I asked more questions and tried to stay on top of things going on in their lives.

By being honest with my children about what happened to me when I finally decided to tell them, they in turn were very cautious and protective of their own children. I have been the designated babysitter for my daughter's children, and if my son's mother-in-law doesn't keep his kids, then I do.

When my kids were growing up, the people in our circle felt the same about protecting our children from predators. We all watched out for each other. If one of us had something to do, we would watch the other one's kids. That way we knew they were safe. What's funny is that all my friends were the same way about their kids. It was like a code; it was just understood because it was something we didn't talk about. But that didn't mean something hadn't happened to each one of us. The main focus was to protect our children and be there for each other during our most fearful times.

I had a Hispanic friend that I was close enough to that we talked about everything. I shared with her about what had happened to me as a twelve-year-old girl. She also shared a similar story. Her family member fondled her, and when she told her mother about it, she said, "Oh, don't worry about it. He does that to everybody. His daddy was like that, too." It bothered her because her mother had thought it was okay.

But you can't keep sweeping things under the rug. Eventually the pile will get very high. As Black American mothers, we will fight to the end if you hurt our babies. But my Hispanic friend said all she could do was not allow this person in her home or to be around her children without supervision. There's nothing unique about her situation or mine—either way we have to forgive the person, or they will have too much power over you and live rent-free in your head. At some point in your life, you will have to serve them eviction papers. I guess it doesn't matter what race you are: molestation, sexual abuse, or rape— all of these things are unacceptable in the sight of God and the law.

The lowest point this fear took me was when I was with my first husband, who is my daughter's father. She was just a baby. I was changing her and saw blood in her diaper. All I knew was that somebody was going to get hurt badly. I had to compose myself because she couldn't talk, so how was I going to know who did this to her? I decided to take her to the doctor before I accused anyone.

When the doctor examined her, he told me that no one had touched her. The baby powder that I used had dried out her skin, and it cracked and bled. I was so glad to know that was the only thing wrong. My husband had no clue that it had almost been a done deal for that brother! I had already plotted in my head what I was going to do to him. I never told him about the way I felt or my suspicions. My mind had been all over the place: because, first of all, who could do this to a baby? Why did they pick my baby? Did they realize that I would fight them? I held everything in even after I came home from the doctor because this would have caused a serious argument between us. I felt bad after I found out he was innocent, so it was good I hadn't said anything.

A person in fear will hurt you badly.

The next lowest point was when my daughter was a teenager, and I found out that she also had been fondled as a child. Since I was always asking questions about someone touching her, she was afraid to say something because she didn't know how I would react. The main issue was that I knew him, which was why she was afraid to tell me. She knew because of my protective nature that I would go after him with all my might. She and I talked about it and came to the conclusion that it would open up Pandora's box if we spoke up about it, so we handled it amongst ourselves and healed together.

The way I moved past this fear was first by talking about it with my children. Communication is a great tool in the Black American home. Years ago, the entire family would sit down at the dinner table and discuss the events of the day; but now, with all this technology, you can sit in a room and not even talk to one another. Kids nowadays say, "Send me a text."

I got through this by talking and praying. The fear has gone about my children because they are grown, but it's always lurking around the corner with my grandchildren. My grandchildren have never asked me why I don't like them to be at other people's houses. They just say, "Granny is old-fashioned and sometimes just old."

Everybody has had some fear of one thing or another. The question is, how do you move past the fear, or how do you overcome this fear? I found out that if I write things down that bother me, put them in an envelope, seal it, take it to the mailbox, and drop it in, it's gone. Sometimes I address it to God or to whomever did me wrong—no stamp, no return address, just nothing. Once I put it in the mailbox it's over. I guess the people at the post office are wondering who it is that keeps writing these letters. It's okay because it's therapy for me. I have also written a letter and then burned it, and after a while, you won't even remember why you were afraid in that situation. Writing this story has been very therapeutic for me because I haven't thought about this situation in years, and I am to the point where I can write and even talk about it without a problem.

If there is anything I would like for you to take away from this chapter, it is to be aware of what situation you are putting your children in. Continue to protect them like a mother bear with her cubs. Communicate with them—make them put the phone down for a few minutes. Turn off the game just to see where their head is. We know our children. Other than God, they are the only ones who have heard our heartbeat from the inside.

If you don't have to, don't leave them alone as much. I was a single parent, and my kids were latch-key children because I had to work. That is true for the majority of Black American women—our children have to mature a little faster. It is called survival. Teach them how to watch out for people who might be trying to do them harm. Show them love. Teach them the difference between a good touch and a bad touch. Teach them how to defend themselves.

Pray that your children develop the spirit of discernment, that they may know who's good and who's not. Take baby steps toward your healing, whether it's God or a therapist or just a friend who really wants to listen and not judge. Your children need to know that you stand in solidarity with them. Don't only communicate but *listen* to what they are saying. Mama is the child's first best friend; they need to know they can come to you when there is nobody else.

Of course, when they are teenagers, you are the worst parent in the world. But I'm here to tell you that they do get over it, you will become friends again, and it's better the second time around. They always need to know that you will protect them by any means necessary. You only get one mom, and they do realize at some point in their lives that you are the best thing since candy.

Prayer Of Healing

Eternal God, my Father, I come boldly before Your throne of grace to obtain mercy in my time of need. Father, I ask that You forgive me for sins seen and unseen. Continue to guide me when I lose my way.

In order to heal, Lord, I'm asking for forgiveness for the person who harmed me. Lord, I ask that You protect my children from all hurt, harm, and danger. Cover them with the blood of the Lamb. Keep them from dangers seen and unseen. Protect them from the hands of molesters and rapists. Protect them from anything that is not of You, Lord.

Father God, in Hebrews 13:5, You said You would never leave me or forsake me, and Lord, I'm standing on Your promise. I'm standing on Your Word, Father God. Lord, I pray for the ones who are still suffering and the ones who are suffering in silence. Father, You said everything that's done in the dark will come into the light. Save those who want to be saved and seek Your face. Open their eyes so that they may see; open their ears so that they may hear the wisdom and the knowledge of Your Word, Lord. Give them the heart to love You and the hands to serve You, Father.

If I had ten thousand tongues, I could not thank You enough. Continue to guide my children and lead them to the path of righteousness. Thank You for always being there for them when they don't know how to be there for themselves. Protect their children and their children's children. Lord, I love You. In Jesus's name, amen.

> *The Lord is my shepherd; I shall not want. He make me to lie down in green pastures: he leadeth me beside the still waters. Psalm 23:1-2*

Chapter **6**

Sticking Out in Greener Pastures

by Chandele Morris

Sticking Out in Greener Pastures

by Chandele Morris

I grew up in a Caribbean American family with a strong belief in getting a good education. Born and raised in the inner city of New York, the majority of people I saw on an everyday basis were Black and Latino. But during the eighties and nineties, in the "Boogie Down Bronx," I didn't have as much of an opportunity to get to know anyone who was Caucasian. When I did, I observed them as something different than what I was used to seeing—except for what I watched on television or saw in most of my dolls.

For me, times of being up close and personal, having conversations, or even being invited into someone else's home were rare, even surreal. It felt weird to me, sort of "out of place," like seeing your teacher at the mall as a kid when you're only used to seeing them at school. Those days, the only real connection I saw between Black and white were the rich people in Manhattan and the not-so-rich people in the Bronx, or the minority school kids getting frisked by white police officers, looking for any opportunity to get one of us in the back of their car.

Fast-forward to 2015. I'm married, and it's time to think about my children's future. Do I want them to experience the world the way that I did? Times had changed. The world was becoming more diverse. After my college days, I was a little more used to spending time with different nationalities and cultures, and I had made some good relationships. I had to decide whether my children would be raised in the same education system and environment I had experienced growing up—which, to me, seemed great at the time. I just didn't want my children to grow up with what I felt was a "crab in a barrel" mind frame, where we couldn't have a nice car in our neighborhood because someone would key it, break into it for coins, or steal its wheels. I didn't want to deal with the possibility that our children could get beat up by a group of kids just because they wanted to be different, or that I would be the one in danger from trying to protect my children because other children's parents had the same mindframe. We realized that if we stayed, our children would be forced to go to a school district with very little resources—where the teachers were burned out, unmotivated, underpaid, and unappreciated, and our children would be the ones to pay for it.

We decided it was time to take the steps to move out of the city so that our children would have the opportunity for a higher quality of education. We moved and reality hit. We were not in "Kansas" anymore. My husband I were the minority in a new town…and so were my children. And in these "greener pastures," we were the ones sticking out.

My Deepest Fear

As a Black American mother, my deepest fear was raising my Black children in a world that might not truly accept them. That fear heightened after George Floyd's death. Of all of the Black killings in the U.S., that one hit closer to home simply because the world started to openly show its true colors.

In 2020, as the pandemic raged on, my children were preparing to join a new school. My brilliant five-year-old son started to have extreme challenges with the constant transitions and expectations in his kindergarten classroom. He would have such anxiety about going to school, and he would escape from the classroom anytime he felt overwhelmed and then cry hysterically when things were not as perfect as he hoped. He became aggressive at times and would throw things off the classroom shelves and kick the wall and even try to hurt himself when he was too frustrated. At times, he was inconsolable and would even run away from school staff who were trying to help him.

A school counselor called me for help with my son, and she had to restrain him to keep him safe and in the building. He had such a hard time regulating his emotions, and no matter what they tried in school, it just wouldn't work.

And then, our brilliant kid was diagnosed with level one autism. I was devastated, and so was my husband, but we really didn't understand autism. We were so caught up in the label of it and the reactions of people around us. We didn't know what to expect or what it meant for his future. I feared that he would grow up and be targeted or disregarded. I worried that his emotional outbursts might continue to adulthood, that people wouldn't understand him and be quick to judge.

I feared that with this diagnosis, all the things I saw in the media—children getting arrested at five years old and autistic Black adults being treated unfairly by police officers who didn't understand—might be the same outcome for my son, my beautiful boy. I figured that, as a Black mom, I wouldn't be enough, and with my limited knowledge of his diagnosis, I thought I would fail him. I wanted to make sure he had the best opportunities available for him and that he would not be dismissed because of his challenges. I needed to be sure that his behavior wouldn't be judged harshly because of someone else's implicit bias. The questions plagued my mind each day: Would he be aggressive and cause someone to call the police? Would he be forced into the most restrictive classroom environment? Would he one day have an emotional meltdown in school and be suspended?

I worried each day, hoping that his "special needs" wouldn't make him stand out too much and that he wouldn't be handled by someone who didn't have patience for a little "Black kid." In New York State's education system, Black students are suspended at more than four times the rate of white students, and children as young as five have been handcuffed and removed from school by police officers because of their challenging behaviors. This scared me to my core because I knew my son's struggle and worried that they would not see his need but instead see his color.

This crippling uncertainty seemed to slow my stride and put a wrench in my confidence as I sent my children to school each day in a community of people who didn't represent people like us and were different from what I was used to.

Each day that I received a call from the school, I wondered if they were treating him with the respect due to everyone. They were quick to tell me that they thought my son belonged in a special ed classroom, which consisted of fewer children, even though academically he proved to excel beyond his peers. Every day I kept my phone near me, dreading to see the number of my children's school pop up on the screen. My heart seemed to sit higher in my chest, hoping that my newly diagnosed, autistic five-year-old old son didn't have a meltdown that caused someone to look beyond his age and decide to call a police officer instead of a counselor. Sounds crazy, but it was happening all over the United States. News articles were popping up left, right, and center. My once strong faith was tested and tried, and I couldn't shake it in a world that now felt freer to be racist. I would not have my children be pushed into the preschool-to-prison pipeline. I refused to let them go that way.

As a mom, you teach your children not to be afraid, but to be curious about the world. We always loved to explore together. But I also had to teach my children to remember that they have darker skin and that their innocent curiosity could be mistaken as threatening. I found myself being hard on my seven-year-old daughter and really getting upset with her for standing too close to the shelves in the store as she tried to read something. She cried because she was simply curious about how the item was made. But to me, I had to see my beautifully curious baby girl in a way that others may have viewed her at that moment—as a possible thief. The same day I rewarded her for trying her best by buying her favorite candy, I scolded her because she put it in her pocket instead of the shopping bag after it was purchased. Other eyes turned to see if we were doing something wrong. It broke my heart any time I had to remind her of how things may look to others because of what we looked like.

Everyone's dream is to have a nice comfortable home in a good neighborhood. As parents, we have the additional wish of finding a great school district. But that wish may be weighed against how racist a community may be and how much we may be accepted. This, of course, always affected our family tremendously because it meant that our resources and opportunities would be limited. Moving to a new area would determine whether my children would be able to walk freely around a store without eyes following them or if they'd receive the same treatment as the next student in their classroom.

Although it was evident that our community also experienced times of uncertainty, I would often find myself wondering how other Black Americans were living. I wondered how other families were dealing with their children. Did they ever ask themselves the same questions that I had? Did they ever have to second-guess themselves, the teachers, the police officers, or even people in the supermarkets? Did they ever have to give their children pep talks to prepare them, just in case they were treated differently or in danger of never coming home?

Many families had been "blending in" for a long time, but I felt a camaraderie, an understanding, and a universal pain with all the Black families I came in contact with after the death of George Floyd. Neighbors who I considered friendly started to hang Confederate flags and yellow flags with snakes, marked "Don't Tread on Me." Colleagues who I was once close to became overly offended and defensive. I even had to be careful with the people I was already comfortable with because I wasn't sure what was truly in their heart.

My lowest point was when I began to second-guess myself as a parent. I knew that as a mom I had to discipline my children if they got out of line, but some forms of discipline I didn't really agree with—especially for a child who was diagnosed with autism. It didn't help that my background was in education where I wouldn't dare hit a child. I was torn between nature versus nurture. I had to reevaluate myself as a mom—a Black mom—and I wasn't quite sure I knew how to do that. I found myself hesitating to make decisions pertaining to my home life, my work life, and even where we would live or send the kids to school.

I felt insecure and helpless because no matter where we moved upstate, no matter what school we put our children in, I would constantly question the reasoning behind decisions school officials made in regard to my children, especially about my son. The question plagued me: Was my son even really autistic, or was that a label they put on him because of his skin color, like so many other Black boys?

Listening to my family and friends of color really put me in a place where I had to rethink my acceptance of other people's words. I had to rely on what God was showing me in my son, rather than the people around me. The schools were pointing out his challenges, some of what I saw on my own; but my family and friends were quick to say that all he needed was "a good pop on the behind" and that he would "grow out of it." I didn't know who to trust. I just wanted to help my son.

By the grace of God, I found myself at a turning point, where I was able to have more confidence for myself and my children. I noticed that my son's school was trying so hard to give him whatever resources he needed. God opened my eyes to the blessings that He was giving me in the midst of my fear and anxiety. I found myself so caught up in what could happen, what would happen, and what was happening everywhere else that I wasn't paying attention to the mysteries of God and all that He was actually doing for me and for my family. I failed to see how God was protecting my children. I was so focused on all the negatives in society and the things that I saw on an everyday basis with many other Black families that I did not see the favor that He had given to me and my family.

I was praying and praying, asking God to cover us, and I didn't even realize that we were being covered. The place that God had bought us—that particular school with those particular people and their experiences—was all orchestrated by God. I started to see the connections of how God was working behind the scenes. He put like-minded people in my path, and people who shared some of my experiences. He softened some hearts before my children got to where they were. They were able to show us that they truly cared about both my son and daughter. They worked hard together to understand my son and look for ways to help him succeed.

I was vigilant to not mention my fears as a Black mom because I felt that they would not and could not possibly understand and may even be offended. But God understood. He knew my heart. What I didn't think about was that He was there personally for my children as well and knew their fears. God was not just orchestrating things for me; He was orchestrating things for *them* because He was also *their* God.

In order for me to start to overcome this fear, I knew I had to trust God to be there when I couldn't. I had to trust Him to be there even when I *could*, and I had to rely on the peace of God to give me the confidence I needed. My mother always told me that God doesn't give us more than we can handle. He has given us the children we need and has created us to be the parents that our children need. "For I know the plans I have for you," says the Lord, 'plans to prosper you and not to harm you, plans to give you hope and a future"(Jeremiah 29:11). I believe this with my whole heart, and I believe this for my children as well. I know that God has a definite plan for our lives, and as long as I continue to pray for my children, God will help me to have peace to know that it's going to be all right. I might waver in my faith—I'm human, after all—but I know I have to trust God's plan even when I don't understand it.

As a mom, my first priority is my children and to make sure that they have the best of what they need. Even if there is no one else around to help, I know that I must be their advocate. Maybe we need to learn a little bit more about what our children are going through instead of looking for professionals, who we hope will help but we notice are often not helping. Perhaps we need to learn what it is that can help our child. Take a stand. Learn your rights and your children's rights and research resources. Perhaps you can even be a blessing to others.

I want you to understand how easy it is to let fear drive your actions and limit any blessings God may have for you. Situations in life may be challenging, and there may be legitimate reasons for concern, but if you trust in the Lord, He will give you peace. He will show you favor. He will prepare a feast for you right in the middle of your enemies. You may end up going through the fire, but when you have faith, you will see that you are not being burned. He will always be with you—just like he was with the three Hebrew boys in the Bible as they stepped into the fire. There is nothing that is impossible for God. Step out in faith and trust God to take care of your family. If things don't go according to your plans, just know that there is a blessing in the storm. You may not understand the process, and your tragedy may feel like your ending, but just know that it is a major ingredient in your blessing. God has the blueprint, and He will give you the tools that you need.

My Prayer

Father God, it says in Psalm 91:4 that You will cover me with Your pinions, and under Your wings I can seek refuge. God, may Your faithfulness be my shield and defense. Give me the strength to walk straight, even when I do not see the path clearly. Help me to stay in Your perfect will and trust You, God. Lord, I know that we can be a people void of love. We harm each other and mistreat each other, but I know that in spite of it all, You love me.

God, I pray that You would give me a sense of peace like no other. Lord, give me peace beyond all understanding, and when I feel alone, let me feel Your presence so that I will be reminded that I am never alone and that You will never forsake me. God, thank You for where You brought me from. I thank You even for all the trials and tribulations that I've been through.

Lord, I thank You for Your perfect will. Lord God, only You know what tomorrow holds. Lord God, You say that the plans that You have for me are plans for good and not evil. So, Lord, when I am in the fire, remind me that You are with me. Send Your angels to be there with me, God, and let me not be burned. Help me to be strong enough to have faith when I'm in the fire, when I'm in a tough time, when I'm in the storm. I thank You, God, for allowing me to take leaps of faith, even when I'm afraid. I thank You, God, because You know what my tomorrow holds, and even when I feel too afraid to take the next step, You still love me and You're still providing for me.

When I felt too afraid to make any moves, God, you ordered my steps. Thank You for allowing me to be the mother that my children need. I appreciate all that You are doing in my children's lives. I know that You love them. I know that Your will for them is better than my will, God. I know that You know their tomorrow, and I know You know the Grand Master Plan. Even when there is something that I don't understand that might not be what I want, God, I know that You have a reason for it. Help me to trust in that. Help me to trust in You.

> *For I, the Lord your God, hold your right hand; it is I who say to you, "Fear not, I am the one who helps you." – Isaiah 41:13*

Chapter 7

Won't God Do It?: Trusting God to Keep His Promise

by Leslie Ann Jack

Won't God Do It?: Trusting God to Keep His Promise

by Leslie Ann Jack

To any Black single mother who harbors the fear that her son could one day become affiliated with a gang, I write this story to encourage *you*. If such a fear is not your reality, then great—don't even entertain the thought! But if it is, I hope that my story can help you to overcome that fear. My every experience thus far has led me to the conclusion that fear can be very limiting, and to give into it will only hinder your growth as an individual.

When I made the decision to migrate to the United States, it took courage, and as I look back, I'm thankful that I was able to swallow any fears that would have surfaced as I endeavored to charter a course to lands unknown. But this does not mean that fear did not seek another avenue from which to plague me. As a parent, I was a target for fear, and it eventually took aim and struck. It has not always been easy, but I have conquered fear, and so can you.

Don't ever allow your fears to take the lead, but rather, let your steps and choices be directed by God.

I read once that fear is false evidence appearing real. What does this really mean? Simply said, that thing that you are fearful of will more than likely never manifest in your reality. It may never be your story. It is a falsity that is trying to appear real, and if you feed into it by giving it more energy than it deserves, it will become bigger than it really is. Believe it or not, most fears are imagined, conjured up by our minds when we give in to doubts and worries that we may feel about situations that are beyond our control. If we were to place our fears under a magnifying lens, we would see that there really isn't anything there.

This is what happened to me. My story is about how I feared that one day I would lose my son to "these streets." I came to America with the hope of creating a life filled with better opportunities for me and my son. I came before he did, having left him with my mother with the intention that I would set myself up first before he came to live with me. Although I knew that my mom would willingly take care of him for me for as long as it took, I needed to have my son with me—he was my firstborn, and I missed him terribly.

Also, as great as my mother was, it was my belief that neither she nor anyone else would have been able to raise him the way that I wanted. I had already envisioned the type of man I wanted him to become, and I wholeheartedly embraced the responsibility that God had placed on my shoulders when He gave me charge of this child. I looked forward to raising him, and I knew that I would relish every moment that I had with him.

He was six years old when he finally came to live with me. Those two years that I lived without him were exceedingly difficult for me. Having him with me made my world come together. But as a single parent, I had the added pressure to meet all financial obligations on my own, and as it was, I was not working for a huge amount of money. However, I was armed with determination; I would do whatever it took to achieve my dreams for us. I had to work long hours at multiple jobs. Having him with me meant that there were periods of time when I was not with him, and it was at this point that my deepest fears began to take root. As a single mother raising a Black boy, I became painfully aware of all the possible disadvantages such a dynamic could give rise to.

I had originally migrated to the United States from a twin island republic in the West Indies called Trinidad and Tobago, where, had I remained, I would have had an entire village to support me. I now found myself in a new environment, away from my family and friends, in a country where everyone seemed as though they were always busy. Thankfully, God sent the right people at the right time to offer me help when I needed it the most. Nevertheless, at the time, I still felt as though I was doing it all alone. In hindsight, I really wasn't, but fear and uncertainty can sometimes distort your vision and cause you to not see a situation for what it truly is.

Any scenario with fear as its driving force can only invite negativity into your life because, unfortunately, that's the way fear rolls. I have always believed in God, but by coming to America and having to raise a Black boy on my own, I quickly realized that saying I believed wasn't enough. My faith in God had to transcend to another level, and I really needed to learn to trust Him. I had to trust Him to hear my prayer and answer it. I felt as though my son's life would be solely dependent on God answering my prayers.

The fear that my son could become a member of a gang had me so uneasy that it affected my ability to parent him. In fact, it wasn't long before I realized that I was instilling unhealthy views about friendship to my son, but I didn't know what to do differently. All I knew was that I had to keep him safe. In my mind, every new friend that he made became a potential enemy because they could be the one to introduce him to the gangster lifestyle. In my efforts to control the situation, I might say things like, "Friends will carry you and not bring you back"—a colloquial saying that we used in the islands, which meant that the very friends who may have invited you along with them would abandon you at the first sign of trouble.

Another rule I implemented was that he wasn't allowed to have any friends come over to our house unless I was at home, and he in turn wasn't allowed to go to his friends' houses under any circumstances. Yes, you could say I was a bit crazy like that—he had no life outside of school activities and wherever I took him.

Thinking back, I didn't always have this fear. It only began to manifest itself when I started to listen to talk within my community about gang activities, information which seemed to be backed up by the media. I would hear news headlines about a boy being killed by a gang of young men, or about women being attacked by yet another group of boys, or other similar stories, and I became even more scared about gangs and gang-related crimes.

I vividly remember someone saying that most of the kids who belong to gangs come from single-parent homes. This caught my attention. *Wait! What?* My kid is in a single-parent home. I zeroed in on this school of thought and quickly accepted it as truth. In my defense, I was naive enough to believe it then, but I know better now. Remember what I said earlier about false evidence trying to appear real? If you allow yourself to believe that because you are a single mother raising a Black boy he is somehow doomed to fail, you would be buying into a lie. That does not have to be your story.

While having to deal with the fear of your son being potentially influenced to join a gang may be a concern shared by any parent who has a son, I am certain that it takes on quite a different perspective for a Black family in comparison to other families. I say this for a couple of reasons. As incomprehensible as it may sound, being part of a gang has been normalized in some Black communities. It has, in some circles, been accepted as a rite of passage that all boys must embark on their way to manhood, when in truth, gangs are destroying our communities. This complacency and acceptance are not being seen among other ethnic groups.

And then we have to also take into consideration the bias of some police officers, who are willing to take the lives of our Black boys without a second thought. Sadly, this goes for Black boys in general, whether they're in a gang or not. I have borne witness to the fact that there are many non blacks who have committed crimes and lived to tell the tale. Our Black boys are not always so privileged, and if they do survive to make it through the legal system, they're not met with the same compassion shown to nonblacks. Our boys are guilty until proven innocent, while nonblacks arrested for the same crimes, in the same criminal justice system, are given the benefit of being innocent until proven guilty. These are harsh truths that can keep a mother awake at night.

Wrestling my fear became an uphill-downhill battle for me, but my lowest point came one summer night when I came home from work and found my son playing outdoors. It was the height of summer, so although it was 8p.m., it was still bright out. But I was so upset that he was still outdoors at that hour that I struck him. Just imagine: My child was only playing with the neighbors, but my paranoid mind, thinking and expecting the worst, led me to overreact. Looking back at the situation, I acknowledge that I should have handled it differently. I'm not excusing my actions, but that's what uncontrolled fear does—it exacerbates things. It was the first and last time that I struck him.

He was at this time in middle school, and as parents, we know that this is a pivotal time in their social and mental development. They are so impressionable at this age, and when I took into consideration the fact that there were no male influences at home, I felt the added pressure to somehow exert my influence over him. I found myself being forceful with him. My voice had to be strong. I had to be the one he feared above anyone else. I figured if he feared me, no one else would be able to intimidate him because I would be the scariest person he knew. How disturbing is it that anyone would want their child to fear them? Especially knowing—like I do now—that having his respect would've produced the desired result.

Looking back, I guess I was not the most fun parent. But things changed for the better just as he started high school. A conversation with my son changed my perspective. One day, I asked him if he had ever been approached by any gang member, and he responded with a yes.

I was caught by surprise. *When did this happen?*

Oh, my goodness! You mean this thing that I had feared the most had manifested itself without my knowledge. Really? How had I missed this?

I immediately followed up with some more questions, like *when, where, how,* and *what!*

He told me that he had been approached in middle school.

Can I tell you something? That school was the last place I feared anything bad would ever happen to my son. It never crossed my mind that he would have been confronted with such an invitation at school. You have to believe me—that school was amazing. The teachers were hands-on, and parents had open-door access to both the teachers and the principal. The entire faculty was great.

How could gang-related stuff be happening there?

It just goes to show you that even though you may try your best as a parent to provide a safe environment for your child, there will always be things out of your control—mitigating factors that you cannot foresee.

I continued to question him. "What was your response when you were asked to join?" I asked.

He replied, "I told them no."

Okay! I asked, "What did they say?"

He said, "They laughed at me, made some jokes, and walked off."

I then asked him if he wasn't afraid to say no, and he said he wasn't.

I began to reason within myself, wondering why he wasn't afraid. I came up with a couple of reasons: Maybe the kid that had asked him was someone he had been friendly with. After all, they had all been together since kindergarten. Or could it be that God had heard my prayers. Either way, only one word came to my mind at that moment: *Whoopee!* I continued my fact-finding mission. The door was opened, and I had to know everything.

"Were you approached just that one time?"

"No." He was asked a couple of times.

I then asked him why he had said no, and his response was my turning point. He said, "Mom, most kids join gangs because they feel as though they lack something from home."

"Something like what?" I asked because, in my head, he did lack something at his home. His dad!

"Things like love, attention, safety, and a voice," he said. "Mom, I don't need to be in a gang. What can they give me? I don't lack anything. Gang members disguise themselves as family who will be there for you. I'm good. I have all the family that I need."

And there it was. It was time to let go of this fear—the monster had shown up and gotten crushed. It was at this moment that I was able to overcome my fear. But it didn't end there. I began to evaluate everything that I had done and said up to that point, and I saw the errors that I had made. Experience is indeed a great teacher, and I would really love it if you would learn from my mistakes rather than repeat them.

One of the biggest truths that hit home for me was the realization that I had not been teaching my son to take note of a person's character. I had made rash judgments about his friends without even trying to get to know these kids or their families. Also, I had neglected to teach and encourage him to trust his own judgments and to be confident in his decision-making skills. What I had done had only served to prevent him from forming healthy, meaningful friendships.

I had to lighten up on my son and myself. I made a quick turnaround. I reduced my workload so that I could spend extra time with him doing things he enjoyed, while allowing him the freedom to be himself and do things on his own. I had to trust my son; I had done a better job than I even knew. My son truly was a good kid, who had proven himself to be not only responsible but also remarkable. Proud mommy moment!

I also had to trust myself and my ability to continue to parent this wonderful young man. I would like to encourage every single mother who is reading this story, and even those of you who are not single parents, to trust yourself on this parenting journey. Regardless of your circumstances, God has chosen you to guide and nurture this child, and He has equipped you to do so. You may not have all the answers, but you know Someone who does.

And this leads me to my most important epiphany: I had to trust God to do His part. I recognized that I had been praying for years but hadn't really had the faith to believe that God would have granted me what I had been asking Him for. God had heard and answered me, but I had not trusted Him to deliver, so I kept asking for something that He was already doing. I had to worry less and trust God more. As the saying goes, "Why worry when you can pray?" Think about it, I had been overly stressed over something that ended up working itself out just fine. This experience has given me a better understanding of what it means to trust.

God continues to care for my son. He has his dream job with a reputable engineering company while he is completing his degree as an engineer. He also gave his life to the Lord.

Won't God do it? Yes, He will. I would like to share my prayer with you as I encourage you to trust God to guide you on your parenting journey. You don't have to do it alone.

Prayer Of Wisdom

Heavenly Father, I come to you as a single mother, charged with the task of presenting society with a healthy, balanced Black man. Lord, I trust You to hear and answer my prayer. God, Your Word tells me that You will be a father to the fatherless and that You will never leave me nor forsake me. I'm taking You at Your Word. I know that I am not doing this alone; You are walking alongside me. Heavenly Father, before I ask anything of You, I first thank You and praise You for Your faithfulness to me and my family. You have brought us this far, and I trust You to continue holding us in the palm of Your hand.

Like Solomon prayed, I too pray for wisdom to raise this son that You have given me.

I pray to have a heart full of understanding, love, and compassion for him. May I always prove to be a safe place for him, that he may be able to trust me with his deepest concerns. And when I don't have the answers, direct me to the ones who do. Father, as I come to You, I am confident that You will help me. For I know that my help comes from You, the Lord, who made heaven and earth.

Father, help me with Your guidance as a single parent to be supportive, encouraging, and corrective in love. Whenever fear arises, help me to remember that it's only false evidence appearing real and to rest assured in the knowledge that You have not given me a spirit of fear. So, in the mighty name of Jesus, I receive strength, power, and soundness of mind.

The enemy does not have a hold over me or my family. In Jesus's name, I pray. Amen. Thank you, Lord.

> *The Lord is my strength and shield. I trust him with all my heart. He helps me, and my heart is filled with joy. I burst out in songs of thanksgiving. -Psalm 28:7*

Chapter 8

My Saving Grace: A Mother's Journey to Finding Inner Forgiveness and Faith

by Deborah Corea Carrington

My Saving Grace: A Mother's Journey to Finding Inner Forgiveness and Faith

by Deborah Corea Carrington

*L*et's picture a fifteen-year-old girl in New Jersey. How would you envision her life? You might visualize an awkward teen going through puberty in her freshman year of high school. Or you might imagine a rebellious coming-of-age story—a child just beginning to make sense of the disoriented world around her.

Based on personal experiences, you may think of a happier time or a depressing time. Some of you might have dealt with bullying and low self-esteem issues. Others may have lived as the embodiment of a popular child prodigy to look out for.

No matter how you think about it, you would almost never associate a fifteen-year-old girl with motherhood and the responsibilities of an adult.

Well, that's the story I'm here to tell. Giving birth at fifteen is not just a story; it's the life that I have lived. You may have already realized that it couldn't have been a walk in the park—far from it. But you may not realize that the gravity of the situation is even heavier for a pregnant teen who is Black and also an immigrant.

Now, I wish to walk you through my journey, to not only share my experiences and struggles but also to help any soul out there who might be feeling alone on their own path. Life is not easy on anyone, and unexpected challenges and turns are a part of it. Sometimes we foresee these challenges, but other times they completely catch us offguard and reroute our perceived journeys.

My story began in Trinidad, my home country. I was the eleventh and last child of my parents. One can imagine what being the youngest of eleven children feels like. No matter how old I grew, I was still the "baby" of the family. Though I started my journey in Trinidad, my life really took flight when I moved to New Jersey. Coming from a relatively conservative family that held Christian values at its core, coming to the United States was a whole new experience.

As a teenager, it was even more challenging to balance between adjusting to the new environment and not uprooting my cultural and religious values. I became sexually active at a very young age when you look at it from the perspective of a Black Trinidadian family. Since the topic was still taboo, Black families didn't really talk to their children about birth control or safe sex. Unlike white children, we were unaware of how to indulge and explore our sexualities without making a life-altering mistake.

Being a young mother was extremely difficult, but all these added pressures that I felt lowered my self-esteem even further. On some occasions, I was way too hard on myself than warranted. That is why I'm sharing my story, so people who feel alone and stuck can know that there is light at the end of the tunnel. Since I grew up religious—and I still hold Christian values at the center of my life—I had to deal with conflicting emotions and a distorted sense of self.

On the one hand, I was going to church and listening to the preaching that said pre-marital sex and giving birth to a child out of wedlock was a sin; while on the other hand, I was the one participating in the same activities. The guilt about this stayed with me for a long, long time, even as an adult. I condemned myself for one mistake I made as a child, and that held me back for so long. Deep down, I believed that I had sinned in the eyes of the Lord, and that made me unworthy of any good thing in life.

The period of pregnancy was one of the toughest times of my life. I could feel my body changing and expanding every moment. Since I was at an age when my body was still in the process of developing, it made the pregnancy more complicated. I was unaware of how to take care of myself and what to expect. Everything was stressful, and I felt so alone. I could not reach out to my friends for advice or even share my struggles because they were all so far removed from them. They were still children in school, while I had suddenly transformed into a "grown-up" with responsibilities.

That period of my life felt like the fastest rollercoaster in the world, and while it went down, it met an abrupt barrier that halted it on the spot. That was how my fifteenth year in life felt. At the time when I should've been worrying about SATs and choosing my courses, I was worried about childcare and support. When I should've been taking care of my own body and growth, I had become responsible for someone else's healthy body and growth.

I went through several emotional swings every day. I would quickly go from depressed to excited to anxious. From the perspective of a young teenager, the entire period was very confusing. I would also feel angry about what had happened to me. There were days when I felt like I was the only one responsible for the situation I was in; but on other days, I would blame everyone but myself.

Becoming pregnant at fifteen caused me emotional turmoil that affected me in ways that I could not have foreseen. I started to see myself as a failure, mainly because I felt like I had let my parents and my community down. My parents had worked so hard to provide a better life and a stable environment for me to get an education and progress farther than them. Instead of making the most of it, I felt like I'd made the wrong decision by becoming sexually active at a young age. I was an impressionable teenager, and for the sake of looking "cool" and "fitting in," it felt like I had compromised my values. I would constantly overthink these things, and then I would feel like I had let myself down more than anything else.

This fear of being a teenage mom also affected me because I wasn't prepared to become a mom at that time. For a long time, I couldn't even foresee or picture myself in the future. All the goals and dreams that I initially had felt unattainable. It almost felt like I had lost the will to live. Every small chore and self-care act felt like a burden. I was unable to understand what was valuable in life anymore. I distanced myself from my friends, and I dropped out of school. It felt like I was completely alone on the path that I had stumbled upon. If you're in a similar situation, you'll be able to empathize. However, let me just say that no matter how difficult and unconquerable a challenge it feels to be now, you will persevere.

The pregnancy finally reached its conclusion after a laborious period, and I was suddenly a mother to a baby girl. To say that I instantly fell in love with the baby that I held would not be an exaggeration. For all my apprehension and confusion during the pregnancy, I suddenly felt a strong urge to protect this baby at all costs and give her the best life possible. Having her made me feel like I had found my purpose in life. All the anxiousness I felt during the pregnancy vanished as soon as she came along.

Slowly yet steadily, I felt like life was making sense again. I found my ground and created a new life for myself. I began to understand that even though this was not something I could've ever anticipated or imagined my life to be, it was still a life that I needed to be grateful for. The Lord works in mysterious ways, and He had blessed me with something that changed my life for the better.

The journey of motherhood had its own challenges. I could not only think about myself anymore because there was another life that was attached to me. I couldn't be reckless or careless with my decisions because they affected my baby girl. In the process, I became a more responsible person. Through motherhood, I came to know myself better. I learned what I found important in life, and I also learned how to love deeply, truly, and completely selflessly. I had the support of my family through this time, and that made me appreciate them even more. Even though I had initially thought I wouldn't be accepted, I was embraced and life went on. I also felt closer to God, and it reaffirmed my faith.

As a young Black mother, I still had a lot of fears about ruining my child. I did not want her to repeat the same mistakes that I had. I wanted to be there to guide her at all times. Over the next few years, I had two more children and a family to call my own. As a Black mother, my deepest fear while raising my children was the thought that history might repeat, that they may have to go through the same challenges I had and make the same mistakes I had. Even though I had come out on the other side as successful, I didn't want my children to go through the same.

My fear was mainly stimulated by the research and studies that I read. Statistically, children born to teenage mothers were most likely to become parents during their teenage years, and the pattern could keep repeating. This knowledge became a nightmare for me and turned me into a strict parent. I was always worried about my children getting into bad company or indulging in unhealthy and risky habits. I loved them more than anything in the world, but that also put me in a state of heightened fear.

I did not want my daughter to follow in my footsteps. I wanted her to do better and thrive in the life that she chose. This constant fear turned me into a restrictive parent. My scrutiny reached a level where it felt like I was robbing my daughter of the simple pleasures in life that young kids need. I didn't realize it at the time, but I was isolating her and not letting her do the things that kids are supposed to do at that age.

Things like sleepovers at a friend's house, going to the mall with her friends on the weekends, and going on dates were prohibited for her. I had such a deeply ingrained fear of my daughter becoming pregnant at a young age that I couldn't see what I was doing to her. My actions and demeanor as a strict mother put a massive strain on our mother-daughter relationship. She stopped sharing her feelings with me and quickly grew distant. I made her feel anxious and on guard all the time. There was also no way for me to explain to her where I was coming from because I thought she was too young to understand the struggles of a young Black mother.

I still vividly remember when my daughter started dating for the first time. She asked her dad for permission instead of me. She also shared the news of having a boyfriend with her dad, and he was the one who told me. It was clear that she didn't trust me or didn't feel comfortable enough to come to me first. That broke my heart in ways that I didn't think were possible. It was then that I started to look inward and tried to see what had gone wrong. I prayed to God and asked for forgiveness.

I slowly began to realize that I was turning into the same kind of parent that my parents had been. I also realized that most of my friends and the people in our community scorned young pregnancy. Since I had lived that reality, it was even more evident to me that this was something that no child should have to go through.

In the Black American community, putting your child on birth control is equivalent to giving them consent to have sex. Unlike nonblack families, who openly discuss these topics and take sex education seriously, we would avoid these discussions. Instead of sitting with our children and addressing the inevitable when they first start dating, we just put unnecessary pressure on them.

This fear made me dictate my daughter's life and made me project my own fears and shortcomings upon her. I remember one day, I asked myself, "Debs, what has your daughter ever done to make you feel so insecure about her?" This question truly opened my eyes and forced me to see that I was expecting my daughter to fail because I failed. Instead of putting my trust in her and coming down to her level to create an understanding, I was just shoving my misconceptions on her and expecting her to obey me. I was so paranoid after finding out about the statistic of children following their parents' paths that I became blind to everything else.

I was expecting my daughter to make the same mistakes as I had because I did not develop trust in our relationship. Then I realized that, although I was scared for her, that one mistake had also turned out to be a blessing in disguise for me. At that moment, I realized that I was hurting my child emotionally, and I was robbing her of her personhood and the experiences that are so essential for a child. This realization made me feel like I had failed as a mother. My beautiful daughter had only wanted to be a child, and I was taking that away from her. I realized that I couldn't control her life always and that I had to come to terms with the fact that she was growing up and she had the right to make her own decisions.

After coming to the realization that my actions were toxic, I came to understand that it was not only affecting my personal life but also my children's. Being a woman of faith, I had to first ask God for forgiveness because I knew that my past and current actions were against His teaching. God said to "Judge not lest ye be judged." He also said that only the one who is without sin may cast the "first stone." This revelation wrenched my heart, but it also worked as an eye-opener for me. For the first time in my life, I understood that I was also sinning against God.

With the help of meditation and the reading of spiritual quotes and inspirational affirmations, I was able to empower my mind to let go and let God lead me through my healing process. I also worked on changing my mindset and my actions in order to heal profoundly. This forced me to take a deeper look at my fears and understand where they were coming from. It became an essential part of my healing from my past trauma and the guilt that was associated with being a teenage mom.

I took some time to self-reflect and look at my life through a lens of kindness and empathy instead of guilt and hatred. I started participating in self-discovery activities and changing the way I saw myself, my children, and the outside world. The healing process was long but worth it. I had to become a better person not only for myself but for the sake of my children. To give them a healthy childhood filled with happy memories, I needed to change my ways and not repeat the mistakes that my parents made. I promised myself that I would be the one who breaks this cycle and paves the way for trusting and healthy relationships.

The reason I wanted to share my story was to help other moms, specifically Black and teenage moms, not fall into the same pit of guilt and self-doubt. While I know that becoming pregnant wasn't on your to-do list as a teenager, it did not defy who you were as a person and who you are today as a Black woman and mother. This was just an event that took place, and you are no different from anyone else. It's important for you to allow your children to live, laugh, grow, and make their own mistakes and memories. To troubleshoot their own problems and gain confidence while doing so will allow your children to become responsible and confident.

It's important for us as moms to empower our children by providing them with the knowledge they need and by letting them experience their own successes and failures. It is our job to pray for them and to cover them under the Word of God daily so that they are always protected by the anointing. Always remember that God did not give us a spirit of fear but of power, love, and a sound mind. Put your trust in God and your journey; they will not lead you astray. You also need to trust yourself and your own parenting, and that will allow you to trust your child.

Eventually, I was able to live a beautiful life with my beautiful family. I worked as a newborn care specialist for twenty years, and then my family and I established a children's boutique that I manage to this day. The power of Black women and mothers is within all of us, and we just need to trust and nurture it.

Prayer For Wholeness

Heavenly Father, Creator of Heaven and Earth, I lift Your name on high. I am asking You to direct my path, Lord. I am weak, but You are mighty. Hold me in Your powerful arms. Father, I ask You to heal my broken heart. Help me to look past the mistakes I've made. Lord, I carry the burden of guilt and shame. Deliver me, O God.

I offer my children to You. I ask You to place Your hedge of protection around them. I bind every generational curse from my bloodline and their father's bloodline. I ask you to wipe away my fears of history repeating itself in my children's lives. I am thanking You in advance for great things to come in my life. Father, I declare my daughters and son are blessed beyond measure. Thank You for setting us free. Thank You for Your healing power in our lives.

Lord, I pray for all mothers, but specifically for teenage mothers: Let Your glory manifest in their lives. Let them know that they are not alone, that it will get better for them if they believe and work toward their goals and dreams and if they surrender it all to You. You, who are mighty to save and strong to deliver, help them to be still and know that You are God. Amen.

"May the God of hope fill you with all joy and peace as you trust in Him, so that you may overflow with hope by the power of the Holy Spirit" (Romans 15:13).

Now faith is the assurance of things hoped for, the conviction of things not seen. Hebrews 11:1

Chapter 9

Shattered Yet Anchored: My Faith Kept Me

by Marlene Asseivero

Shattered Yet Anchored: My Faith Kept Me

by Marlene Asseivero

*G*rowing up as a young girl in the West Indies, my parents weren't religious, but they did teach me and my siblings the value of right and wrong. The home was filled with laughter, joy, togetherness, and some rebellion. Our father was very protective of his five daughters and son, but one thing he made sure of was that we knew we were loved. Love was the center of our family. My parents took the time to teach us the value of family, relationships, friendships, and religion. Even though our parents were strict, we were still allowed to express our feelings, and when they felt we were walking in disobedience to the rules of the house, it led to table discussions. Everyone's opinion was valued and mattered.

As you can see, my family foundation was loving and fair with a strong emphasis on moral values. Many of these values still resonate with me today.

At the age of twenty-one, I gave my life to Jesus and said yes to Him ruling and reigning in my life. During this time, my father also committed his life to Christ. By choosing to seek and follow Christ, our home was transformed, even in such habits as language and routine. My parents added a Christ-centeredness to our home—prayer, worship, and the Word of God.

I would attend church and return home very late due to lack of transportation. My father would remain awake until I arrived. I can recall many times opening the door and hearing him call my name to make sure it was me. When I responded, he then said he could go to sleep. One day I asked him why he did not just go to bed when he wanted. He said, "When you have children, you will understand!"

Now being blessed with the gift of being a wife and a mother to three amazing children, I can relate. I now know why my father never went to bed until we were home safely, why we were never allowed to have sleepovers unless he interviewed the parents first, why the person we were dating could not stay at our house past a certain time, why I was never allowed to pursue my athletic career because the distance was too far to travel. I did not know that those same fears that my father felt were embedded into me until I found myself implementing them on my children. Even though my oldest two are now married, I still find myself being fearful for them, but in different ways.

After my son visits and when he's leaving to go home, I often wonder if the cops will stop him because of his sports car. *Will they both have successful marriages? I ask myself. Will they remain faithful to their spouses? Will their spouses remain faithful to them?* Even when the youngest says, "Mom, I am getting a ride with my friend," my heart often flutters, and I will not rest until he's home safely. Why that fear? Because there are so many accidents with young drivers. Or perhaps they are pulled over by the cops, and my son, who's very outspoken, says the wrong thing at the wrong time. We are living in a society where social injustice and racial profiling is high among Black American men, immigrants, and those of different ethnic backgrounds. Here, you can't seem to drive a nice car or accomplish great things because of the color of your skin.

My eighteen-year-old son recently graduated from high school, but before then, he encountered institutional racism in the healthcare industry. Someone may ask what institutional racism is; it is a form of racism that is embedded through laws and regulations within a society or an organization. It can lead to such issues as discrimination in criminal justice, employment, housing, and healthcare. In healthcare, many patients are unfairly profiled and denied care, drugs, and referrals. Dr. Monique Tello, contributing editor of the Harvard Health Blog, recently pointed out that "it is well established that Blacks and other minority groups in the U.S. experience more illness, worse outcomes and premature death compared with whites."

My son, who I will refer to as MJ, started high school and had a desire to play football. At the age of fourteen, he was already six feet tall, and his body was built like a much older adult. My husband and I never wanted him to play that sport, but after careful consideration, we permitted him to try out for the team. After MJ completed the tryout process successfully, he made the junior varsity team. All the while, we were fearful of an injury or a concussion. Although spiritually we knew the Lord would protect him, naturally we knew the severity of the injuries that could arise.

Needless to say, he was doing something he loved. One day in September 2017, he invited the family to come to one of his games. During the game, we noticed that he was moving in a very lethargic way. Suddenly, something felt wrong within me. A knot arose in my stomach that only a mother gets when she knows that one of her children is hurting. The other players thought he was being lazy and was no longer interested in playing. But why would he throw away his dream? I knew that wasn't the case.

Once we made it home, he was still expressing an intense level of pain. My husband and I purchased multiple medications to help relieve his muscle pain, but none of them seemed to get the job done. At that very moment, I knew that MJ's life was about to shift drastically.

That one injury affected him academically, physically, and mentally. What he was once capable of doing on his own was now a tedious task. He needed assistance with dressing, support with walking, a lift when entering and exiting a vehicle. He needed help toting around his backpack, and he was not able to stand for a long time. The hurt and sadness I felt for my son were unbearable. Being in high school and not having the ability to move around like other high schoolers was not an easy exercise. It became depressing, and after bringing his condition to the school's attention, he was allowed to use the elevator on campus to get to and from his classes. In addition to that, a student was assigned to help him with transporting his class materials and backpack.

After receiving needed assistance with maneuvering around campus, MJ's schooling began to decline. The medication that he was prescribed was causing him to be drowsy, and he was not able to remain engaged during class. Since elementary school, MJ had been in the gifted program, but the unfortunate situation of his injury caused his grades to decline.

Can you imagine on a scale of one to ten the level of pain I was experiencing as his mother? I had to witness my son in pain both physically and academically. We scheduled an appointment for MJ to see the doctor. He was assigned a female physician who was new to the medical facility. Dr. K. informed us that she was not experienced with the procedure for helping him recover from his injury. Due to her lack of experience, MJ had a longer recovery process. This led to continued feelings of despair and frustration.

After making several attempts to get the medical treatment that he needed, we encountered bureaucracy. After an x-ray, doctors discovered a bulging disc and scoliosis, which led to a limp. We put in a request for a referral to see a doctor who specializes in sports injuries. Eventually, that referral was given, but after several sessions, the situation was deemed untreatable. He was given a special sole to place inside his shoes for height. That made him feel very uncomfortable, unhappy, and dissatisfied. MJ felt that his situation had not been given enough attention, and he had been cheated out of proper medical care. Eventually, he was sent to a chiropractor for physical therapy, but by then, the damage was already done.

As a pastor and a mother who believes in the power of prayer, I could not believe that this had happened to my child. Once again, my faith was tested, but I had to be strong for my son. I had to believe that this situation could change for the better. Believe me when I tell you that I still believe in God for the complete healing of my son. If it never happens, I will still trust and believe that God has a plan and a purpose for this tragedy. For I know that the Lord makes no mistakes.

MJ was smiling and laughing normally out loud, but silently he had become emotionally disturbed—even entertaining thoughts of suicide. So, you can only imagine my expression when my son verbalized those words to me: "Mom, you know I wrestle with suicidal thoughts." I was in shock that this was happening to the pastor's son. The pastor who prays for others to witness signs, miracles, and wonders! Now I question how I missed it. Was it because I took it for granted that he was being raised in a Christian home? He was surrounded by love; we prayed and read the Word together. *Can this be happening to the son who I raised to love and fear God?*

Well, let's face the truth—even as a Christian, a pastor, and a mother, the harsh reality is that mental illness is real, and many families are affected by this illness. Please never allow any conversation to be too hard to discuss. I had to learn how to be comfortable having uncomfortable conversations. This is something that we have to address, both spiritually and physically. There is the saying that it takes a village to raise a child; I needed to find outside resources to assist in reaching my son. So, I secretly consulted with his guidance counselor to reach out to him. His siblings and other young men in the church became his mentors, and they rallied around him because the fear of losing him to suicide would have been too much to bear. As fate would have it, MJ had to eventually return to the same healthcare facility for an appointment, and who would be the physician present that day? Dr. K. Upon seeing MJ, she apologized to him and said that a day doesn't go by that she doesn't think about him and the decision she made not getting him the treatment he needed sooner. I don't know if it was my son's situation, but she eventually left that practice. I must say a hearty thank you to the community of support that stood by MJ—his dad, siblings, church family, teachers, and friends—for giving him the strength to persevere and to silence the deadly voices that were speaking loudly in his ear.

After consulting with his new doctor, he was given the good news that he can return to sports; but he would never be able to play football again. MJ has found a new passion for sports again. He's competing in javelin and shot put, and he recently placed third in the state championship for shot put and seventh overall in javelin. As a pastor, woman of God, mother, and intercessor, I had to put all those titles aside and be the mother that my son needed. There is a verse in the Bible that declares, "Lo, children are a heritage of the Lord: and the fruit of the womb is his reward" (Psalm 127:3).

This was the son of my old age, and I was given a responsibility by the Lord to take care of him. With that said, I want to encourage you: Don't ever stop fighting for justice, equality, and greatness for your seed(s). It does not matter our status in life, whether it's pastoral, educational, entrepreneurial, and so on. A parent's first responsibility is their children. Let them know we see them and that they have first place in our lives. In our own ways, we all know how to pray, so keep praying the changes we want to see will occur when we unite together as ONE. Let us become relevant to our generation by raising our voices for truth and justice.

As a Black mother, I overcame my fears by solely putting my trust, confidence, and faith in the God of my salvation. I knew that this battle was too much for me and I needed His divine assistance, so I prayed, fasted, and read His Word. By doing so, I received the peace I needed to overcome this hurdle. His Word also reminded me that He promised never to leave me, neither would He forsake me, and He would be with me always. Knowing that He didn't give me a spirit of fear, but of love, power, and a sound mind, I truly trusted and believed in the God who had brought me this far.

Whereas this was my outlet for dealing with my situation, I want to assure you that there are many groups and organizations that can help handle any type of crisis. None of us have to handle it alone. Reach out to a loved one or someone that you trust in your inner circle. Share your concerns, hurts, fears, and vulnerabilities with them. Another reason I kept this matter private was because I didn't want to be judged by society. Seeing that I am a pastor and the world expects me to be perfect and strong, I had to remind myself that even Christ was judged, and He was perfect in every sense of the way. I am just a mother trying to live right and to be the best example as a wife, mother, friend, and pastor. So, with that said, please let us not judge each other, but let's demonstrate the love, care, and support that we all need on this journey of motherhood.

A Prayer from a Mother's Heart

Father, in the name of Jesus, as I come before Your throne, I want to express my appreciation for all that You have done for my children. Your love and grace are amazing because they have brought them thus far, and I know they will continue to keep us a family—whole, safe, and sound.

Your Word declares in Matthew 16:19 that whatever we bind on earth will be bound in heaven, and whatever we loose on earth will be loosed in heaven. By the authority that is in Your name and Word, I bind up every attack of the enemy that brings distraction and distractors to derail us from Your plan and purpose for our lives. In Jesus's name, amen.

Thank You, Lord, for shining Your light into the hearts of those who are suffering or who are battling with any form of sickness or disease. For Your Word declares that You are touched with the very feeling of our infirmities. Thank You, Lord, for Your healing touch. For by Your stripes, Jesus, the broken, wounded, abused, and given-up are healed.

Father, in the name of Jesus, I join my faith with all the other mothers who are trusting and believing You for the miracle, healing, breakthrough, transformation, salvation, and deliverance of those we care about. We stand on Your Word "that the effectual fervent prayer of a righteous man availed much" with You, God. May we also experience Your healing power, so we can become a beacon of hope and light for our families and communities.

As women/mothers who believe in the power of prayer, the spirit of unity, and the bond of peace, let us continue to stand in the gap for each other, by praying, raising our voices, and lifting each other up, so we all can become overcomers and victors.

Blessed is she who has believed that the Lord would fulfill his promises to her!" Luke 1:45

Chapter 10

A Story of an Immigrant Mom Raising Her Children from Afar: Overcoming Fear, Guilt, and Anxiety

by Tanisa Newby

A Story of an Immigrant Mom Raising Her Children from Afar: Overcoming Fear, Guilt, and Anxiety

by Tanisa Newby

*H*ave you ever given thought to the way that history tends to repeat itself? As I contemplate my life and the direction it has taken, I can't help but think of the irony. Sometimes you can self-righteously judge someone and feel justifiably validated in doing so. But, as has been rightly said, you can never know what a person is going through until you have walked a mile in their shoes. I say this thinking about my mother, who in her quest for a better life migrated when I was an infant, leaving me in the care of my grandmother and aunt. My father unfortunately had been killed.

Although all my material needs were met, and she did her best to maintain communication with me, it wasn't enough. In those days, we wrote letters, as cell phones did not exist. Being a sickly child, I felt like I needed her more than I needed anything else, and I greatly longed for that motherly comfort that only she could have given. But it never came. I grew up feeling emotionally disconnected from her.

Back then, try as you might, you could not have gotten me to understand my mother's decision. But now that I've found myself in the same unenviable position of having to leave my kids behind, I can see things clearly. Sometimes life can throw you unexpected curve balls, and all you can do is put your foot forward and hope for the best. My mother did just that. In the face of adversities, she did what she had to do to survive, and now I was doing the same.

But at that time, all I knew was that I missed her, and nothing else made sense. I felt alone and rejected, and at one point I thought I might have resented her. And now, here I am, many years later, a Black immigrant mother. Like my mother before me, I had to make the decision to leave my children in the care of relatives as I headed out in search of a better life for myself and them.

Like a scene in a movie, I envisaged myself standing at the very crossroads my mother would have stood at with uncertainty so many years ago, desperately wishing for a compass that could point her in the right direction. Although the circumstances that brought us each to this crossroads were different, our motivation was the same. We wanted the best for our children.

My journey began when, in my mid-twenties, I found myself the single mother to three children under the age of ten. My husband and I had separated within five years of being married, and the separation had been hard and bitter. He was a vengeful person and did everything possible to make my life difficult. He withdrew all financial support from me and my kids and became an absentee father. During our marriage, we had both been employed, but his salary had been larger than mine.

When we separated, I was barely earning enough to pay the bills, much less put food on the table. At the end of each month when I received my salary, I would often have to choose between paying my landlady our rent or keeping the electricity on—not forgetting that I also had to figure out how to fulfill my other financial obligations. I had outstanding loans to repay—recurring expenses related to my health, as I had been diagnosed with an acute kidney disease that would sometimes relapse, requiring me to be on medication for long periods of time. And last but not least, I bore the full responsibility of providing for my children.

My struggle was real. Very, very real! Although I was resilient and determined to learn how to manage on my own, I felt as though I was fighting to keep my head above the water. I knew that I had to find a way to rise above my present dilemma.

As I sought to build a new life for myself, the Lord began to open door after door, and He sent the right people into my life to help me. I gratefully accepted every bit of kindness shown to me as though I was being handed a lifeline. One of those doors opened the way for me to migrate.

Having to leave my kids behind was one of the hardest decisions I've ever had to make in my life. They were the bedrock of my existence—my reason for living.

But here I was starting this whole new life, and they were not with me. And though I was excited that I had been given this opportunity, I was terribly afraid about what I could lose in the process. I feared that my kids would grow up feeling abandoned because they were young and tender, and both their parents were absent from their day-to-day lives.

First their father had left, and now I was doing the same. I knew that they were bound to feel rejected, and I expected them to develop deep-seated resentments toward me and eventually lash out. I convinced myself that they would eventually grow to hate me and not allow me to be a part of their adult lives. In my mind, I could already picture not knowing my grandchildren. I had heard enough stories from children who had been left behind by their mothers to know how far those feelings could go. In fact, I, having been a casualty of such a situation, could safely vouch for their feelings. I had felt the same.

As a young child, I could not understand how my mother could leave me behind. In my eyes, it had seemed as though she had left and never looked back. It didn't help when mean adults would glibly say things like "Your mother forgot about you." I can also attest to wrestling with feelings of rejection well into my adulthood. Without warning, they would rise up, setting off all kinds of hurts and pains. To be honest, I hadn't ever wanted to confront those feelings until now.

Finding myself walking in my mother's footsteps and anticipating my kids' emotional response to having their world turned upside down finally brought me to this place. I believed that my own past experience would give me the insight to see things through my children's eyes. Like me at their age, they too were having to make the adjustment to not having both parents physically present in their lives, and I knew that it was going to be rough. Even though I knew I was doing my best, I also knew that to them it wouldn't seem like enough.

Regardless of what I said or did, they were going to feel neglected, abandoned, and rejected. Nothing could have been further from the truth, however, and I intended to reinforce that every chance I got. But I knew too well the power an ill-spoken word could have upon their impressionable minds.

I was afraid that their childhood would be tainted by that feeling of being left behind. It became my greatest fear: that my children would believe that I had abandoned and rejected them and that they in turn would reject me. I couldn't allow that to happen.

But I couldn't put these thoughts out of my mind. Every waking moment I was consumed by my fears. I constantly found myself having to deal with internal battles that left me struggling with conflicting emotions, sometimes second-guessing my decision, questioning if the financial gains were even worth the upheaval my kids were going through. I tried to weigh my past against their future as if to decipher how much it had played a role in things being the way they are now. I felt like a gambler—I could throw the dice and win, or I could lose. In my heart of hearts, I felt as though the odds were against me.

Sometimes, to escape my thoughts, I would try to unwind by doing something exciting like going to a fancy restaurant or simply walking in the park. Yet even then, my thoughts would be on my children, and I would find myself ether thinking that I shouldn't be having fun without them or wishing that they could be there with me. I was so overwhelmed with grief from missing them and knowing that they were missing me that I battled daily with what they call "mommy guilt."

I found no reprieve. I felt engulfed in hopelessness. My spiritual life plummeted. I became depressed, lost interest in everything, and gained a lot of weight. The fear of my kids rejecting me made me do things that I normally would not have done.

I tried to overcompensate by giving them everything that they asked for and by sending them money often. But in my heart of hearts, I knew that this was a poor substitute for what they really needed. And I really did not want them to grow up with the mistaken belief that their affection could be bought.

My fears were mine, but I knew that it touched my children, as I was unconsciously seeking validation from them. It was as if I needed to hear that they understood why I had done what I did and that they knew I was a great mom. They would have sensed my frustration, and this only added to theirs. On the flip side, I had supportive family members who were very instrumental in caring for my kids, ensuring that they never went hungry or missed school. While I was grateful for this, I knew that those things would not be enough. Sometimes tensions would flare because I could be a little overprotective.

Don't misunderstand me—there was no question in my mind that my relatives cared for them. I trusted them to take care of all of their physical needs, but it was their emotional well-being that troubled me. I often worried that they would not be shown the compassion that their circumstances warranted. There were also times when I felt it necessary to stand in defense of them and their points of view. This, of course, would sometimes spark controversy.

The bittersweetness of life often got to me. In those days, I worked as a nanny, as I have a natural love for children. There were moments while caring for my young charges and showering them with love that I would think of my own kids and my inability to do the same for them.

Fortunately—or unfortunately—I wasn't alone. There were other immigrant mothers, nannies like myself who I would meet on playdates, and we would sometimes share how challenging it was, attempting to parent our children from afar. This proved to be quite therapeutic. Trust me, it's never good to keep your fear bottled up. Talking with these ladies helped me a lot, and I felt less alone. They too had found themselves in circumstances where their socio-economic status left them with no other choice but to leave their children in their home countries in pursuit of a better life. And like me, they had to grapple with the emotional issues such a decision entailed. We were all aching in our hearts for our children.

As a Black single mother, working with Caucasian families and witnessing the wholesomeness of their family life, I could not help but think about my kids and what they were missing out on by not having both their parents with them. I thought about their dad and the stance that he had taken, choosing selfishly to not be actively present in their lives, in comparison to the men in these families I worked for.

These fathers were very active, attentive, and supportive in the lives of their children. I was also thrown by the fact that these grown men unashamedly displayed love and affection to their children, hugging and kissing them openly. This is something I wasn't used to seeing in my upbringing. I had never known a father's love, but I had desperately wanted this for my children. In the world that I came from, men did not show affection, they didn't carry their emotions on their sleeves, and they most definitely didn't cry in public. To do so was not considered manly.

Our Black men had to prove their manhood by being rough, tough, and gruff. I thought about my kids' father, and I prayed that he would somehow have an epiphany and become the parent that my kids needed him to be. I was trying my best, but they needed him to step up to the plate and do his part. I had never wanted to be a single parent, and although this breakdown in family life was not reserved for Black families only, it was very common, and the children were the ones paying heavily. In the Caribbean, it had become quite commonplace to hear about single Black mothers migrating in search of opportunities to take care of their families. And there have been just as many stories trickling down the grapevine that forewarned that, while there were some advantages to this, there were disadvantages as well.

Parental absenteeism often led to children acting out, becoming juvenile delinquents, being preyed upon by voyeurs, or worse. Plus, most kids rebel in the face of perceived rejection, and this can be very destructive to the parent-child relationship in the long run. I didn't want my children to be carrying around emotional baggage because they felt abandoned by their parents. Black people, both male and female, are already notoriously labeled as hot heads whenever they have an emotional response—even in the instance of a natural reaction—and I didn't want my kids to ever find themselves in a position where they fit any such stereotyping. My children's voices would be heard, and it would evoke commentary, but for the right reasons.

It wasn't long before I began to see signs that gave credence to my fears. My eldest and my youngest at first acted as if they had it all together. But then they started saying things like, "If you were here, this wouldn't have happened," hinting at their discontent.

My second child, however, was the one who had me tossing and turning, as he was showing all the signs of a kid who was depressed. He was acting out his frustrations, showing signs of resentment and intense aggression. His grades were also dropping. Desperate to stop his downward spiral, I arranged for him to receive counselling sessions, in the hope that it would help him. But the final determination was as I expected—he wanted to live with his parents. But my hands were tied; circumstances didn't allow for me to return home.

I continued to be afraid that he and his siblings would grow further and further apart from me. One day, I was thinking about my mom and how I felt when she had left. I thought about how she had tried to maintain communication with me by her letters, and I felt a tug in my heart. I thought about the fact that in those days we didn't have the technology that we had now, but even so, she had tried to keep those lines of communication open. I thought about how I dreadfully missed my kids, and I remembered how sometimes it was the simplest things that meant the most. It hit me that I was wasting valuable time wallowing in fear.

I didn't have all the answers, but there was one thing that I knew for certain: I loved my kids. And although we were separated by distance, my love could bridge that gap. I determined then that I would be an active participant in their lives. I wouldn't allow them to feel rejected. Let them push me away if they wanted, but I would do all that I could to be very present in their lives and ensure that our relationship was solid.

I reconnected with God. My prayer life got a jumpstart as I listened to sermons and gospel music. I also started fasting as a part of my healing process.

Forgiveness is key.

I forgave my mother for leaving me behind, recognizing that she had not done so to escape being my mother, but because she was my mother, she loved me, and she did what she had to do to take care of me. I had been looking at my situation from a skewed perspective. I had only ever seen things from my point of view, not hers, and that wasn't fair. Our relationship since has blossomed, and we have grown wonderfully close.

I also realized that I had been operating under the assumption that my children would see this the way that I had seen it, and in doing so, I had opened the door for my fears to become my reality. But I had caught myself, and I would not leave any room in their mind for doubt.

Thankfully, technology has its advantages, and we made full use of it, hanging out and shopping together online. I even assisted them with their homework. I reminded them how important they are. I sent them daily love messages, and I made sure that they knew that the plans I had for the future would always include them. Their trust and confidence in my love for them grew, and my kids and I are closer than ever.

To those of you who will read my story, I want to encourage you to:

LIVE fearlessly. Life doesn't always go as planned, but where there is life, there is hope.

LOVE boldly, without fear. Love freely, knowing that true love is given with no strings attached—it cannot be measured, nor can it be restrained by time or distance.

LAUGH in the face of your fears. It's the best medicine to soothe your soul and will be as music to the ears of those who will rejoice with you when you have overcome.

And always keep the lines of COMMUNICATION open.

A Prayer When You're Overwhelmed and Need Strength

Dear God,

I come to You today with a humbled heart. Thank You for watching over me, for watching over my children, for watching over my family, for watching over all mothers—our Black mothers who are experiencing fear and trauma and self-doubt and sadness in their lives. Encourage our spirits today, Lord.

Lord, give us the strength and patience that we may need to overcome our struggles—the struggle of the mind, Lord; the struggle of the heart, Lord; the struggle of the spirit, Lord; the struggle of the body!

Holy Father, I thank You for helping me day by day, step by step, especially in moments when the guilt of the past or the weight of the present feel overwhelming. As Your Word reminds me, "When my heart is overwhelmed, lead me to the Rock that is higher than I." Just then, I will lift my eyes unto You, God. You are my Rock, Lord; You are my strength, Lord; You are my protector and my provider, and I will continually trust in You.

Give ear to the words of my heart, Jesus, and give comfort to my soul, and grant me the peace that passes all understanding as I carry on this journey—not just for myself but for all those I can help along the way.

In your sweet and precious name, I pray. Amen.

> *But the Lord stood with me and strengthened me,
> so that through me the proclamation might be fully
> accomplished, and that all the Gentiles might hear;
> and I was rescued out of the lion's mouth. 2 Timothy 4:17*

Chapter **11**

Breaking the Chains: Combatting the Effects of Alcoholism in the Home

by Irina Curenton

Breaking the Chains: Combatting the Effects of Alcoholism in the Home

by Irina Curenton

I couldn't contain my tears. Rushing to the upstairs bathroom and quickly closing the door behind me, the tears fell like a rain shower in a never-ending stream, and I fell to my knees. This was the second time I'd rushed to the bathroom, and just like the last time, the tears just kept flowing. Curled up in a ball, I sobbed uncontrollably for a good ten minutes straight.

Was this kind of pain really worth it? Did I have the strength to endure another round of this kind of soul surgery? How much more of this did I have to go through before I *finally* got my breakthrough? Yet even as these thoughts rushed through my mind, I still knew I had to endure this too. I'd come way too far in this journey to stop now. I felt the presence of God resting upon me, and I heard these words in my spirit:

> *Felt the pain sharp and deep,*
> *All I could do was weep.*
>
> *Joyless and alone, I couldn't force a smile,*
> *Not realizing I'm surrounded by love all the while.*

Some days may feel tough,
Though He carried my burdens,
On that rugged cross, this road is still rough.

Let healing come,
Let Your will be done.
I will trust You through this maze of joy and sorrow.
I'll make the best of this day,' cuz I wasn't promised tomorrow.
(Irina Curenton—February 5, 2018)

Flashbacks

The memories kept flooding back. "No, Mommy! Not again! Please don't..." I thought to myself as my little heart sank. By now, I knew what would happen. Helplessly, I stood by, watching the woman I adored so deeply start her daily drinking cycle. But it was too late! There she sat, downing one tall, clear glass after another, until she passed out. With each drink, I felt her spirit slip away further and further, becoming more and more inaccessible. She looked lifeless and distant, sitting there in the kitchen, and it scared me. Out of desperation, I tugged at her shirt, trying to get her attention, but she seemed to not even hear me. So I tugged harder. As I frantically called out for my mother, her face changed. Enraged that I'd disturbed her, she screamed at me with a voice unlike any I'd ever heard before, and I froze in fear. I was almost five years old, and I felt helpless and scared.

I didn't understand what had just happened. All I was trying to do was get her attention. I wished so desperately that she would play with me. But I didn't know how to get through to her—how to break down this invisible wall that seemed to barricade her heart. There were so many questions I wanted to ask, like why was she mad at me? What had I done wrong? Why did she have to drink like this all the time? Why wouldn't she just stop? Did my mommy still love me, and if she did, why didn't she play with me? Why did she choose those bottles over me? *Maybe I'm not worth it,* my little mind reasoned, and since I kept it all in, there was no one to challenge my thoughts, and they began to build a well-traveled pathway.

*   *   *

As these painful memories flooded my mind, I felt like I was reliving the trauma, and my body stiffened. My shoulders tensed, and my heart raced. I felt fatigued from the many years I'd walked through my personal wilderness experience, and I didn't know how much longer I could keep this up. In that moment—between the present-day stressors of kids and housework, on top of building my business and facing the past—a strong urge to drink suddenly came over me, and for a split second, I entertained the thought. Couldn't I just numb the pain instead of walking it out? Wouldn't it just be easier to give in?

Finally, I understood the struggle between flesh and spirit, and why she had chosen to give in.

Living in Chaos

Excessive drinking was a regular occurrence in our house. Chaos reigned: house a mess, clothes piled up all over the floor, kitchen sink full of dishes. I felt overwhelmed just looking at the mess all around me, but I didn't know what to do about it. Confusion, frustration, irritation, and uncertainty were constant companions. It was hard to know what to expect, where the lines lay, and it felt like the rug was pulled out from under me so much that I came to expect it. I started living in a constant state of anxiety and fear, dreading the times when my mother drank. Yet, faithfully, she drank bottle after bottle, fully engrossed in her thoughts while pushing me away. I felt very alone.

By the time I was eight years old, I felt myself having lost all hope that things would ever change. Occasionally, she'd send me to the Wine Cellar to pick up more alcohol for her after she ran out. I absolutely hated going. I remember one evening in particular. It was almost dark, and I was terrified of the old pervert who roamed around our quaint, small-town neighborhood, looking for little girls who were lost or alone. But I knew I had to go. Thankfully, all went well—except the stress and fear that surrounded me as I made the trip there and back home.

Why Am I Sharing This?

Born into dysfunction, it's been a lifelong determination of mine to break free from the chains of addiction, abuse, and chaos, which I witnessed all too often growing up. During childhood, my heart always longed for loving, supportive family connections. When I became a mother, that desire grew to include breaking generational cycles in my family line so my children would not have to endure the pain and disconnection I had. As I've matured and continued this healing process, God has birthed a vision in me to not only break cycles but to instill new patterns. I want to help other families do the same.

I've had many fears crop up during my journey of motherhood, but one of my deepest fears while raising my sons was that my children would either fall into a pattern of addiction themselves and allow it to destroy their lives or that they would carry the effects of this ugly disease into their future, recreating the same unhealthy patterns in their own families.

Do the Numbers Lie?

Studies show that *one in eight* adults in the United States suffer from alcohol addiction. Globally, it's estimated that 14.5 million people, ages twelve and older, have alcohol use disorder[1]. Among the Black American population, statistics show that although there may be later lower levels of use, Black Americans face greater levels of alcohol problems and are estimated to be more heavily affected by substance abuse and mental health conditions, with the two being closely related.[2] The 2018 National Survey on Drug Use and Health reports that "6.9% of African Americans have a substance use disorder compared to 7.4% of the total population and 3.4% of African Americans have an illicit drug use disorder compared to a rate of 3% among the total population.[3]

For the longest time, I gave way to this fear, mentally entertaining statistics and all the bad things that "might" happen, stressing and focusing on the negative things I saw happening right in front of me. When I saw a close family member start drinking in front of the kids and lose their cool, I was thrust back into the trauma I'd experienced as a child.

What I did not realize at the time was that God allowed this experience to bring the needed healing so that wholeness could reign in my life and I could start internalizing trust at a deep level.

Finding My Tribe

As we walk out our faith and learn to overcome, it's important to share our testimonies with others we can trust, as the Lord leads. Though my circle was somewhat small at that time, I am forever grateful for the people God sent my way to walk out this journey with me on an intimate level. As I silently battled hopelessness and resentment around alcoholism, I had to learn to stand in the midst of what looked like chaos and crisis. For me, it took a lot to get to a place where I could fully trust that the Lord had my children and that He would cover their minds and hearts when they saw loved ones making choices that didn't line up with our beliefs.

Each of us are responsible for our own lives, but having supportive friends and mentors is vital through this process. By His grace, I started connecting with several friends who I found out were dealing with this same fear. Together, we started sharing our fears one-on-one and as a group, praying together, learning how to stand our ground, working on ourselves, and rising up on as we learned to trust God through the process. It was not easy. There were many days we cried, but stewarding supportive relationships and sharing our fears helped tremendously as we started doing our own heart work and allowing the Lord to work out old mindsets in us.

I am so thankful that I knew I wasn't alone, and that I had someone to share my fears with. As I grew, I leaned on my supportive friends more, learning to trust that they appreciated who I was and valued my voice and validated my concerns. As a result, I was able to stand and support my sons in a more effective way, holding them accountable for their own process and learning to trust them to walk out their own journeys. With time, I let go and let God have His way in their lives. I learned how to give grace for mistakes they made and affirm them in healthy ways, while taking greater ownership of my own life and leaving all the things beyond my control to God.

Celebrating Our Differences

I feel like I need to share a bit of my background for you to really grasp my heart and why I'm so passionate about families dealing with heart issues. My experience with alcoholism, and the fear surrounding it, as well as racial tension, is unique in the sense that I am biracial. I have received much flak from both races about the way I look, and I've had to make my peace with who I am and what that meant for me. Growing up with a German mother, who was and is extremely passionate about racial injustice, and a proud Caucasian hillbilly stepfather who had some strong opinions about Black people; marrying a Black American man, who is all about Black history and celebrating our "blackness"; and later discovering my biological father, who is passionate about the history of Black Americans and Native Americans, have taught me to embrace and see all people, no matter their race or nationality, through a lens of love and respect.

In many spaces, I have been the minority. I have received looks of disdain and felt like I did not belong. This is why I treasure my supportive friends, even though for a long time, I felt like I did not fit in, therefore my concerns and fears did not matter. Even in my own home, many times I felt invalidated and unsupported. For a long time, I dealt with a fear of attachment. For me, community was built outside of the home, and I had to learn how to be at peace with who I was and how to build community within my home.

As a mother of young Black men, I've tried to help my children feel like they belong, to work through their emotions, and learn to resolve conflict in peaceful ways so they did not get caught up in the web of addiction. I think often of the aggression and hatred toward young Black men and women and the misunderstandings that have resulted in death. I've feared often that my children would put themselves in the wrong situation at the wrong time and that a decision to drink or use drugs would cause them to let their guard down. While I believe that most mothers have this fear, the reality is that, among Black people, the news of police brutality and the prison pipeline speaks loudly.

My Low Point

When my mom started reliving her trauma and I saw her retreat, I felt my heart drop. Around that same time, we lost a close friend to overdose, and I felt terrified. I saw my life flash before my eyes, and I felt like my whole world—the world I had so carefully constructed and crafted—was falling apart.

It all felt like too much for me to bear. Everything felt out of control, and I was on the edge of a nervous breakdown, worrying about how things would turn out for my boys and how in the world I would protect them from the disease of alcoholism and its effects when it came knocking on our door. Mentally, I was on overload and my thoughts would race often; I had a hard time being still. My fear practically consumed me and caused me to live in a constant state of fight or flight. I often had panic attacks and crying spells, falling apart and crying hysterically at the drop of a hat.

Emotionally, I felt discouraged and weary, and I carried tremendous heaviness in my heart. Depression almost consumed me as I walked in mommy guilt and shame, crying for my kids and wondering how I had not seen this coming. I just could not wrap my mind around the fact that breaking the chains wouldn't happen for me and my family. Often, I felt paranoid and hypersensitive about any sign of addiction manifesting itself, and I sat timidly allowing life to happen to me.

Spiritually, I walked in so much condemnation, unforgiveness, and resentment about the alcoholism and fear that my children would carry on the generational curse that I could not fully grasp Jesus's love for me or understand why He would want anything to do with me. The stress from these fears and resentments was beginning to manifest in my body. Physically, the pain from all the worry and stress showed up in the form of pain, in my back, shoulders, sides, legs, heart, and stomach area. It affected my menstrual cycle, and during one of my doctor's visits, I had to have overgrown polyps removed to ensure they weren't cancerous.

The Turning Point

So, how does one bounce back from something like this? For me, the turning point was two-fold:

1. I realized that I needed to be strong for my boys and family, and I wanted to set a godly example.

2. I was also reminded of the promise God gave me several years before that I would be whole and that I would help to break the generational cycle in my family line. I wanted that more than anything because I knew that as I walked in wholeness, my family would too.

It took a lot for me to acknowledge that I needed help, but God remained faithful and kept wooing me to Himself slowly. In addition to discovering and doing extensive research to educate myself on addiction and recovery, I overcame by making the commitment to do three things daily:

1. Pray, renew my faith, and trust God for things that cause me to be fearful.

2. Seek the support of trustworthy friends, mentors, and counselors. For me that included support groups like Al-Anon.

3.   Intentionally implement and practice tools I learned on a moment-to-moment basis. I incorporated tools like journaling and the try-fail-adjust method.

How to Apply This to Your Life

As you walk out your own healing process, I want to share three tips that you can use to help you overcome your own fear:

1. *Trust the process.* God loves us unconditionally and wants the best for us, so we can trust Him no matter what it looks like. For me, it took thirteen years to get to a place of fully learning to trust Him.

2. *Learn to love yourself unconditionally* so that you can learn to love others well. There is a huge difference in the way that some of us were taught to love and the way that God loves us. Meditating on 1 Corinthians 13 really helped me get a clearer picture of what "love" looks like.

3. *Purposefully PAUSE often.* It is imperative that we pause to reflect as we heal. You can do this through journaling, reading God's Word, and waiting for God's direction. There is great power in the pausing.

Just a Quick Reminder

As I bring this chapter to a close, dear friend, I hope you were blessed and received some practical tools to use in your own journey. I want you to know that generational healing IS possible, and that no matter how much opposition you may feel rising against you, YOU CAN DO THIS! It will require DAILY, moment-by-moment surrendering to walk out this journey, but your family line is worth it—YOU are worth it—and you don't have to do this alone. Find your tribe and link arms together. Be encouraged and KNOW that God loves you deeply and wants you to prosper, even as your soul prospers!

Prayer to Trust God to Break the Cycle of Addiction and Codependency

Dear Heavenly Father,

Thank You, Lord, for Your omnipotence. I stand in awe of You. I thank You that You are BIGGER than any form of addiction and the residue of codependency in our lives. I surrender and lay myself at Your feet. I thank You that You are a very present help in times of trouble. I confess any hurt, unbelief, resentment, bitterness, hardheartedness, hopelessness, disobedience, and impatience to You now, and I ask You to forgive me. Please listen to my cry for help, my King and my God. Hear my voice and move on behalf of my family. Please lead my family in the everlasting way.

You know my heart, Lord, and You see every part of me, and I declare that You are greater than the residue of any and every addiction and codependent behavior present in our lives. I choose to stand in the gap for my sons, that every form of addiction—including alcoholism, abuse, and codependency—is broken in their lives and the lives of their children through the third and fourth generations now in Jesus's name and is replaced with true devotion to You.

Please work into my children's hearts a deep and everlasting love for You, Your laws, and Your statutes, and may their wives and children love You with their whole hearts as well. I pray for Your blessing and favor upon them and their families from this day forward that they prosper in all they do. Every bondage is broken.

In Jesus's name,
Amen.

> *And without faith it is impossible to please him, for whoever would draw near to God must believe that he exists and that he rewards those who seek him. Hebrews 11:6*

Chapter **12**

Blessed Shoulders Don the Capes: Unsung Heroes to the Rescue

by Pamela Wilson

Blessed Shoulders Don the Capes:
Unsung Heroes to the Rescue

by Pamela Wilson

$\mathscr{S}$cience teaches us that everyone is made up of X and Y chromosomes. We learn that a child inherits genetics from both parents. But it is always a gamble as to which genes a child will receive from each parent. Will they have their mommy's eyes and daddy's nose? Or will they have their daddy's height and mommy's stride? Will they have Mommy's gentle spirit or Daddy's temper?

As a parent, you have no influence over the genetic makeup of your child. You don't get the opportunity to handpick the features from you and your mate that appeal to you and build your child to specs. There is no shopping around for genes. You can only accept what is.

As a parent, your sphere of influence lies only in the qualities that you can nurture in your child. It is a known fact that children are products of their environment. They practice what they see and what they are taught.

As a parent to three kids—two girls and one boy—I can say that they are each individuals in their own rights. But I tried to exert my influence over each of them in the hopes that they would be exemplary people when they grew up. But I often wondered how much of a stronger influence genetics would have.

After raising my first daughter for three years in a house full of strong, opinionated, and beautiful women, I then had my middle child, my son. And I asked myself, *What am I going to do with a boy?* This was unfamiliar territory, and I felt this pressing need to get it right. As I looked at him and thought of his father, I couldn't help but begin to look for similarities—not just the physical things that were plainly visible, but I sought to see how much of his father's personality was in him.

My relationship with my son's father hadn't always been complicated. In the years before our son was born, we had a great relationship. We made plans to build a life together. It was only after my son was born that things really started to change. This was partly because I changed. I had my young son, and I worried about the influence his father's life choices could have on him. I began to view his bad habits and criminal past in a new light. I didn't want my son to have to grow up witnessing his father's errant ways.

The birth of our son hadn't stirred him to take concrete steps to change the direction in which his life was heading. I became afraid that our son would grow up and somehow follow in his father's footsteps. I realized that I would have to do what was best for my son. At the time, that meant separating from his father and beginning afresh. I wasn't expecting it, but I felt a huge sense of relief and unburdening when I made this decision. I knew that I was doing the right thing, not only for my son but also for myself.

My son's father missed out on his childhood because he spent most of that time in and out of prison for various offenses, but most often it would be on assault charges. It was his temper that made everything so hard for him and us. I was all too familiar with his temper. I had borne the brunt of it many times. A simple conversation could take a dangerous turn if he felt attacked. I always felt like I was walking on pins and needles, afraid to make the wrong choice or say the wrong thing.

As my son grew older, the fear that he would follow in his dad's footsteps continued to plague me. I couldn't deny what I was seeing. Although I had left that relationship to spare my son from having to grow up in a volatile environment, I saw that nature would have its way. Though I saw bits of myself in him, there was no denying that he was more like his father than I had hoped.

He had inherited his father's rage. When triggered, my son would become so intensely emotional that he would see red, losing all sense of reasoning and unleashing his anger uncontrollably. I was always afraid of what his anger could lead to, especially because of the situations I'd already undergone with his father.

It was as though I was reliving the past that I had shared with his father. Hindsight told me that if left unchecked, my son's anger would cause him to reach the point of no return and spiral out of control. I had to do everything in my power to ensure that would not happen. I would punish him harshly and scold him constantly, thinking that this would straighten him up. At times I felt like more of a warden than a mother. My vision became blurred, and I didn't even see him as my son but as a younger version of his father who, if I could change him, might still have a future with me. I was afraid for my son, I lived in dread of the day when the good that I had tried to instill in him would be nullified by one reckless decision.

For me there was no singular moment of fear; I lived on the edge and carried my fear with me every day. Whenever something happened, whether major or minor, I questioned if this was "the moment" that the train would come off the tracks. Would the way I yelled at him to focus so he could finish his homework or slapped his hand for trying to take a piece of candy before dinner change who he was forever? What was "the point of no return" for a child?

Many people recall the life-changing moment when they lost their way. They speak of that peer who offered them drugs at a party or the coach or teacher who told them they would never amount to anything. But I knew that, even though those events could trigger a setback in a person's life, it wouldn't be truthful to place the brunt of the blame on these alone. Most of the problems that people struggle with as adults are rooted in things that happened at home.

I remember the first time my son went to stay with his father for a weekend; he was around five years old. He was young but still able to communicate. I packed some clothes and snacks in a little bag for his first father-and-son getaway. It was Friday, and his dad would have him until Sunday evening. He came to pick him up that afternoon accompanied by his girlfriend. This threw me at first because I knew this was not what my son was expecting. He believed that he was going to spend some one-on-one time with his dad. Though it irked me, I didn't say anything because I knew he really wanted to go and I had always vowed that I would never keep my children away from their fathers. So, I let him leave with them.

The next morning, they were at the door, his bag gripped in his father's hand like a baseball. My child shuffled past me in the doorway, almost half the size of the boy I had ushered off the day before. His father pushed the bag into my hand, cursing. It looked like a breakup scene from a movie. When I went to my son, he wouldn't speak of what had happened. All he would say was "Mom, it's okay." His silence scared me. Even at this tender age he was already adept at bottling his feelings. My five-year-old looked like he'd become a man in less than twenty-four hours, and I couldn't decipher what was happening.

I had no clue what went wrong. I had worked so hard to build a strong and beautiful child, and it felt as though one night with his father had caused everything to come crashing down, undoing years of progress. How could I fix this? I couldn't keep him from his father but clearly whatever had taken place was destructive. His withdrawal caused my fear to creep in further. My son grew older, and with each passing day this fear did not leave—it grew worse. His father had by then been incarcerated so many times that there was no way that my son could remain unaffected. His increasing rage and his inability to control his emotions made me fear that he too could eventually find himself behind bars.

I kept waiting for the other shoe to drop. I was tormented and frustrated. I found myself having so many regrets that I grew depressed. I also felt angry with myself over my inability to help my son. I began to feel fatigued and stressed. I couldn't even center myself spiritually. I was at an all-time low. I was also concerned about how everything that was happening would impact my other children. My eldest daughter was three years older than her brother, and my other daughter was six years younger. If you asked me, I would say that I love all my kids the same; but if you asked them, they would always say I loved him the most.

Knowing they felt that way hurt my heart. I never wanted my daughters to feel as though they were any less important to me than my son. But I can see how my fears revolving around him could have made them feel that way. They would have seen my concern and worry as extra attention, and as young as they were, they would not have understood what motivated me to be that way with him. I was so intent on pouring as much of myself and my values into him in the hope that it would lessen the degree of his father's influence that my daughters ended up feeling neglected. I had to do better by them all, but I didn't know how.

I felt as though I was all alone on this journey. I was ashamed and couldn't imagine what I had done that caused me to deserve to be in this situation. I was a good person; I had lots of love to give—not only to my children but to others as well. My passion lay in being an inspirational guide to kids who may be battling against the odds. But here I was struggling to get it right with my own family. I knew that there were many single mothers like myself charged with the responsibility to raise successful Black men who would change the narrative of Black men through the ages. But are we equipped to do so? I don't think so—we have our roles to play as mothers who nurture and guide, but fathers have a role to play as well. They are representatives of manhood; their sons are supposed to be able to look at them and see what being a man truly means.

It is to society's detriment that so many of our Black males are imprisoned, sometimes for minor infractions that could justifiably be dealt with outside of the prison system. There is little to no emphasis being placed on rehabilitation and reconciliation. My son was affected physiologically, physically, and socially. His father being a part of the prison system meant that my son indirectly was a part of the system. He too was paying right alongside his father for his father's sins. Had his father been given the necessary tools to manage his anger, he may have been able to work through his issues and spend less time imprisoned.

But Black men are lost in a system that does not take into account the history of oppression that Black people have faced and the systematic breakdown in family that has continued to thrive because of it. That lack of awareness is compounded by misinformation and a fear of stigmatization that have kept our Black males from being able to climb out of the vicious cycle of anger, rage, and bitterness, which, for want of a better outlet, continues to manifest itself as violence in varying forms and degrees. I was trying to break that cycle with my son so that he would not carry this curse into his own future family. There was a real possibility of this happening if I didn't find a way to help my child. I knew this because, as hard as it was for me to admit, I was afraid of him—my son.

One time, his little sister hid the remote when he went to the bathroom because he would not share the TV time. In a rage, he flung her against the wall. When his older sister came to her defense, he pushed her down and broke the bed. The girls had to run out of the apartment to their grandmother's a few doors down for refuge. I had stepped out only a few minutes prior to get some batteries at the store below us. And it scares me to imagine the other possible outcomes of that story.

After scolding him about the situation, he asked me a question that changed everything for me. He asked if I loved him differently. I was flabbergasted! As a mother I felt like I had done everything possible to show my son how much his well-being and safety meant to me, but my child could not see it. He could not discern my love. All he saw was harshness and grit and the hard shell I presented, not knowing that these were the result of my fear for him. All he noticed was that he got in trouble when his sisters didn't, which made him feel isolated and attacked. Again, I'd been doing my best to help my child, but somehow, I had unintentionally pushed him away in the process. I felt like a failure as a mother.

This feeling was only made worse when I learned that he was skipping his classes. I became terrified that he would become a high school dropout, further opening the door to a life of hardship and the possibility of being convicted of some crime.

I found myself asking God to help me in a different way. Instead of a generic prayer asking for provision and covering for me and my children, I sought guidance. I said, "God, You've given me a healthy son. Now please help me to raise him."

I got him into an alternative school, where he was able to get the additional support necessary to get through his classes. I also placed him and his siblings into any program I could access, to keep them occupied and less likely to fall in with the wrong crowd. And I kept on praying, "Guide him, Lord. Help me raise this boy." And God answered tenfold. He sent strong men, who filled the gap left by his father's continued absence by serving as mentors and father figures in his life. My brother, family friends, and church leaders all stepped up to the plate and began to help me mold my son into the young man that he should be, and I was very grateful.

But there was one man who stepped in and molded him in life-changing ways. It was our family friend Jimmy, a construction worker who owned his own business. He took him under his wing during his teenage years, and on days when he didn't have school, as well as during the summer, Jimmy would come as early as 6 a.m. to pick him up and drop him off later in the evening. My son graduated with his high school diploma. That diploma made a big difference in my life. It took away the fear and gave me hope.

I felt as though my son had a fighting chance. It also gave him hope, as he realized that he had what it took to turn his life around and do better for himself. And he did! He began making the right choices by planning for a successful future.

Mothers who are raising children on their own should be commended, but single parenting is not ideal. A child is a product of two parents, and ideally for that child to thrive, all efforts must be made to ensure that both parents are contributing their time, effort, and energies toward nurturing that child. Genetics are important and should not be disregarded, but nurturing is pivotal. You can shape the way your child sees the world; the way they embrace challenges and difficulties; how they process hurts and disappointments. You can inspire them to love themselves, with all their flaws and weaknesses and yet still work on being better.

If you are a single mother doing it on your own, you don't have to carry the weight of the world on your shoulders. A good support system, consisting of people who care about you and your children and can share your vision for them, is not to be sneezed at. When I relinquished my self-appointed job of knowing every answer and having to do it all on my own, I opened the door, firstly, for God to step in and direct my path, and also for those who were willing to throw their hats in the ring and help me on my parenting journey. My fears began to dissipate to the point where I no longer felt as though I were carrying the world on my shoulders alone. My support system expanded, with others lending me their shoulders to lean on, and I gained immense strength from their support.

Mothers are seen as superheroes. Our children see our capes and magic in our eyes. It can sometimes seem to them as though we have all the answers and can make everything possible. You care about what you're doing as a mother, and that says a lot because it means that you do not wear this title lightly. But you don't have to do it alone. I gratefully acknowledge those unsung heroes who have helped me along the way.

As the saying goes, "Heavy is the head that wears the crown," but I'd like to say, "Blessed are the shoulders that don the capes."

Prayer to Order His Steps

Heavenly Father, I come to You today to pray for my child, knowing that I have Your ear. You have given me a word concerning them, and I believe that the words that You have spoken will never become void but will prosper. Lord, You know better than me Your will for my child's life, so I come to You that You may show me the way that I should go. Fill me with all wisdom that I may speak the right words over their life. I ask that You equip my child with knowledge, understanding, and wisdom so that they will make wise choices and that they will grow in favor with God and men.

I pray that You will give my child the gift of discernment that will allow them to tell the right path from the wrong and that You will always guide them by ordering their footsteps. I pray that my child will have a strong work ethic and will do all things with integrity. I am reassured by Your affirmation that my child will be strong and courageous. They will not be frightened or dismayed, for You will be with them wherever they go. Lord, I also hold onto Your blessings and promises that declare my child to be above and not beneath. Thank You for Your love and favor.

SPOKEN WORD

Fearless Not Careless
By Nzinga Fortune

In all things I am walking in His light.
I am fearless only because of His might.
He directs my path.

He healed me from my inadequacy.
He removes all the pain.
He erased all of my shame.

He rebuked all darkness from this heart.
He is my source.
Yeah, the Creator, He is my driving force.

To Him I owe every glory.
I will not live in FEAR.
I will not live in FEAR.

Yea, though I may walk through the valley of doubt and despair,
I will not FEAR because this much is clear:
The Lord is my light and protection—

Whom shall I FEAR? No one!
The Lord is my path and my direction.
Of what shall I be afraid? Nothing!

I was created in His image and likeness—
Melanated skin like copper,
Hair like wool,

A beautiful BLACK QUEEN,
The original Eve, Mother to my brown-skin boys and girls.
Like I said, Fearless NOT Careless.
I'm no superhero, but to my kids, I am their Shero

Because.........

I am Brave in His Glory.
I am Strong in His Mercy.
I am Faithful in His Righteousness.
I am Fruitful in His Blessings.
I am Powerful in His Word.
I am a Child of God.

Conclusion

Dear Reader

Now that you've reached the end of *The Secret Prayer of a Righteous Black Woman: The Power of a Mother's Prayer,* you have heard the stories about how 12 mothers used prayer and other holistic approaches to eliminate their parenting fears and negative thinking. Would you like to do the same?

Our prayer for you as a Black mother is that you discover your maternal purpose and power as you pray for your children and yourself, committing everything to God's passionate protection, and wage war against fear and worry. We want to help you conquer your parenting fears and limiting beliefs so that you can be mentally, spiritually, and physically free.

We encourage you to begin your own healing journey, and to do so, we have created a digital journal—*The Secret Prayer of a Righteous Black Woman: The Power of a Mother's Prayer Break through Journal: Eliminating Fear & Negative Thinking.*

Together as a community of Black mothers, we can do anything. We are praying and rooting for YOU, Sis!

Please visit https://darapublishing.co/breakthroughjournal/ to receive your digital copy today.

ABOUT THE AUTHORS

Reea Rodney

Reea Rodney is a woman of God who lives by the scripture verse Philippians 4:13, "I can do all things through Christ who strengthens me." In addition, she is a wife and mother of three woderful young adults. A resident of Brooklyn, New York, Reea is originally from Trinidad, a small Caribbean island in the West Indies. She migrated to the United States in 2006 in the pursuit of a better life for her family. Being an immigrant made her even more determined to succeed and achieve her American dream, which was to further her education and create a life that was purposeful and purpose-driven.

Since then, she has acquired a Bachelor of Science Degree in Healthcare Management and an Associate's Degree in Occupational Studies with a major in Medical Assisting, as well as several certifications in the medical field. Reea is the CEO and Founder of Dara Publishing, LLC, which is her publishing company, and Dara Wisdom and Empowerment Coaching, which is her life coaching practice. As a serial entrepreneur, Reea holds the titles of Self-Publishing Consultant and Book Coach. She works with aspiring authors to help them achieve their literary success so they can create an impact!

As a Parent and Children's Personal Development Life Coach, Reea has created an after-school program that helps children develop a positive mindset, and she works with students within the New York Public School system and privately in her practice. In addition, Reea is also a Certified Cognitive Behavioral (CBT) Coach, Motivational Speaker, and a #1 Bestselling Author. Over the past four years, she has successfully self-published 20 books via her publishing company and has written 24 Personal Development Modules and 12 Personal Development Manuals for her kids coaching program.

Reea credits all her success to hard work and perseverance, as well as a strong belief in herself and in her purpose. Reea is determined to spread positivity wherever she goes as she believes that we can all achieve whatever we set our minds to while creating a legacy for our families.

To learn more about Author Reea Rodney, please visit her website www.darapublishing.co or email her at darapublishing@gmail.com.

You can follow her on social media at:

Facebook: www.facebook.com/reea.rodney
Instagram: www.instagram.com/reearodney1/
Twitter: www.twitter.com/darapublishing

Fenyx Blue

Bold, Loving, Unapologetic, and *Evolving (BLUE)* are words to describe Fenyx Blue. Ms. Blue is an author (young adult novels Who Failed Johnny? and Battle of the Bullies; children's book Worth the Weight: A Rare Gem; and poetry book The Blue Ink Movement), You Tuber (Fenyx Blue Ink), speaker, ministry leader, mentor, instructional coach, and her school district's former "Those Who Excel" Teacher of the Year.

Ms. Blue speaks to audiences about their purpose and power and works to coach other authors through their journey to become published. Her novels are tools for teachers while being like candy for students. She is a veteran English teacher who has worked with readers K–12.

Ms. Blue created an organization called Team BFF (Bully-Free Forever). Her students have partnered with other schools, marched, and provided education on bullying. In addition, she directs a youth anti-drug program called Snowflake that helps students to solve problems, build relationships, and make positive choices.

With the support of other educators, she developed DIVAS (Daughters Inspiring Values and Sisterhood) to build bonds between middle- and high-school girls and prepare them to be productive citizens. Ms. Fenyx Blue lovingly refers to her squad as neighbors on her YouTube channel because she believes we are all connected in some way. Ms. Blue is the mother of three children, a native of Chicago, Illinois, and loves to travel, learn, garden, and read.

Follow Fenyx @FenyxBlueInk on all social media platforms.

Rhonda Small Peters

 Rhonda Small Peters is the founder of Mount Olive Spiritual Baptist Tabernacle of Praise, which opened its doors in 2013. She is a powerful woman of God—a messenger to herald the second coming of Christ. Rhonda prides herself on being Christ centered and people focused, passionately committing herself to the advancement of God's kingdom.

Outside of her ministry, she is a dedicated wife and devoted mother to six beautiful kids—five boys and one girl. She has also assumed guardianship alongside her husband to his niece, who lost her mother in 2019.

Growing up in Trinidad and Tobago, a small country in the Caribbean archipelago, she admits that her life there was bittersweet, a mix of good and bad times. In hindsight, she attributes these experiences to having shaped the person that she's become and ultimately helping her discover her purpose and define her priorities. Her own early struggles as a single parent have given her insight into the daily battles faced by parents who are raising kids in the face of economic hardships.

This led her to initiate the "Bread Basket Ministry" in 2018, which supplies additional food support and basic hygiene products to needy families. Her personal mission is to wage war against childhood hunger, and her credo is that "no child should ever have to go to bed hungry." Her long-term goal is to assist families beyond the provision of food hampers by formulating systems that would allow for the eradication of poverty through sustainable living and self-sufficiency.

Follow her on social media:

Facebook Bread Basket Ministry:
www.facebook.com/breadbasketministry

Facebook Prophetess Rhonda Small Peters
www.facebook.com/ProphetessRhonda

Michelle W. Fuqua

Michelle is the founding pastor of Living Water Church International and Chosen Ministries, the parent organization of God's Chosen Women. Her life mission is "Seeking His face, pursuing Him with passion, growing in the knowledge of Him, and doing His will," so that others may come into a saving and growing knowledge of God through Jesus Christ. She has diverse experience across Corporate America, holding multiple leadership positions.

Michelle is a two-time bestselling author in the anthologies *Souled Out, Volume 2* and *Soulful Affirmations,* and the author of *Shattered Perceptions,* which appeared in the anthology *Love Said Not So,* and *In Christ We Live: A 40 Day Intimate Journey to Strengthen Your Daily Walk with Christ.* She holds a Bachelor of Science degree in Mechanical Engineering, an MBA, MAR in Pastoral Counseling, and a Master of Divinity degree. She is a candidate for the Doctor of Ministry degree and is currently working on the final project. She is a certified life coach and holds a certificate in Diversity, Equity, and Inclusion from the University of South Florida.

Michelle loves to read and write, and she wishes that she had a singing voice. She coaches and mentors to assist people with clarifying their purpose and the steps needed to achieve it. Michelle's most important ministry is to her family. She is happily married to Louis, and they have two sons, Daniel and Christian.

Follow her on social media:

Instagram: www.instagram.com/michellewfuqua
Facebook: www.facebook.com/michellewfuqua
Twitter: www.twitter.com/michellefuqua

Debra Turner-Ray

Debra Ray was raised on the South Side of Chicago. Educated in the Chicago public school system, she attended Lincoln University in Jefferson City, Missouri, and Olive-Harvey, a city college in Chicago. She is the middle child, with an older sister and a younger brother, raised in a two-parent home of hard workers. That is where she obtained her values and work ethic from at an early age. At the age of 30, she attended Marion Adult Training Center, where she received a certificate as a Respiratory Therapy Technician. She worked in this field for seven years.

When she found out that seven is the sign of completion, she moved on to become a Certified Hemodialysis Technician, which she did until retirement. Debra is married to Clarence Ray. She has two biological children and five bonus children. She and Clarence have 24 grandchildren!

She is the published author of two books that can be found on Amazon. The first is a book of inspirational poems titled *To Whom It May Concern*. The second book, *Why Me?* is a memoir about how she survived drugs, alcohol, and an abusive first marriage.

Debra writes plays and has put on two productions. She is currently working on expanding her brand. She and her family are under the same ministry, since 2010: The Upper Room Outreach Ministry, where Elder Christopher Brown is pastor, and Prophetess Towanda Brown is co-pastor. God is Good. Be Blessed!

Follow her on social media:

Facebook: www.facebook.com/debra.turnerray
Instagram: www.instagram.com/debraray79/

Chandele Morris

Chandele Morris was born and raised in the Bronx of New York. Chandele has more than fifteen years of experience in education, providing services to children and families as a teacher, school director, child-development specialist, and early childhood educational consultant. She received a Master's in Curriculum Development and Early Childhood Education. She is a trainer, a speaker, and an advocate for early childhood educators. Along with being an educator, Chandele is the author of the bestselling children's book *I'm Just a Kid: A Social-Emotional Book on Self-regulation,* which gives a real-life snapshot of what families experience with children who have big emotions.

Chandele is married and has two inquisitive children, one of whom was diagnosed on the autism spectrum and was the inspiration for her first book. She has a passion for teaching children and a desire to relate to parents, which is what inspired her to write a children's book. Chandele spent the majority of her career working in Head Start, one of the United States' leading early childhood government-funded programs that focuses on high-quality education for children from birth through age five. In her career, she was trained to see the best in educators and to motivate them to excel in their practices through professional development, close mentorship, feedback, and support. It was this experience and her knowledge of childhood development in typical and special needs children that led Chandele on the path to find excellence for her own children.

To learn more about Author Chandele Morris, please visit her website www.morrishousepublishers.com or email her at morrishousepublishers@gmail.com.

Follow her on social media:

Facebook: www.facebook.com/Morrishousepublishers

Leslie Ann Jack

Leslie Ann Jack is the second of three daughters, born in the sunny twin islands, Trinidad and Tobago. She currently resides in Brooklyn, New York, with her two amazing, beautiful, and kind children, who are her "WHY" in life. Leslie Ann is determined to leave them a purposeful and enriched legacy.

Having worked as a certified Childhood Development Teacher in Trinidad, Leslie Ann has been a Childcare Specialist for the past 10 years in Brooklyn. Her desire is to influence children in positive ways, that they might grow into confident, well-rounded individuals who see the world as a beautiful place.

Leslie Ann is also a woman of faith who believes that the power of prayer can change any situation. She fellowships at Brooklyn Tabernacle church and serves in the Keepers of God House and Evangelism Ministry. Leslie Ann is also a member of the Daughters of Zion Ministry, a group of women who encourage each other to live their best life, in accordance with the Word of God.

Passionate about serving, Leslie Ann is an NAJ board member, which is a non-profit outreach organization serving communities, churches, shelters, and families, here in the United States and internationally.

Leslie Ann finds joy in the simple things, such as long walks, new foods, and road trips with her family. She lives by Romans 8:28: "And we know that God works together all things for the good of those who love Him and are called according to His purpose."

Follow her on social media:

Facebook: www.facebook.com/leslieann.jack

Deborah Corea Carrington

Deborah C. Carrington was born in a fishing village in the western part of the beautiful island of Trinidad. She's the youngest of eleven children. Her childhood was filled with adventures—mountain climbing, fishing, gardening, and swimming in the ocean. Although these were humble beginnings, it was an incredible experience.

Today Deborah is the mother of three wonderful children, and she is blessed to be grandmother to two beautiful grandchildren. She and her family now reside in Hoboken, New Jersey, since she migrated in search of the American dream in March 1998. Inspired by the endless stories she had been told, that America was the land of hope and opportunities, she knew coming here was best thing to do to achieve the life she envisioned for her children.

Although her early years in America were filled with trial and error, she eventually got her life together, thus living the American dream. Presently, Deborah is the manager for her family's children's boutique, Small Wonders, in Wycoff, New Jersey. Small Wonders is sort of a miniature version of Saks or Bloomingdales, given the clientele it attracts. She has been manager for a little over a year, and she loves it. She never would have guessed that she would be overseeing what she considers to be the creation of her little family's Empire and Legacy.

Follow her on social media:

Facebook: www.facebook.com/Debs07304
Facebook: www.facebook.com/smallwondersnj

Pastor Marlene Asseviero

Pastor Marlene Celeste Hankey Asseviero is originally from the beautiful islands of Trinidad and Tobago, the sixth of seven children of the late Bishop Roy and Fedora Hankey. She accepted Jesus Christ as her personal savior at the young age of 21, and she served with her father in the ministry for 10 years. She eventually met and married the love of her life in 1991. She and her youngest two children would migrate to America in 2000 to join her hubby who was already there as a missionary. There, she gave birth to "the son of her old age," the youngest by 10 years.

She was ordained as a Pastor with the School of Bishops in Brooklyn, New York, in 2002. In 2005, the family relocated to Baltimore, Maryland, with the instruction of the Lord to raise a people high in name, honor, and praise. In 2006, Pastor Marlene and her husband established GACC, where she has served as Senior Pastor for the past four years. Marlene also founded Women of Virtue, a women's ministry that believes every woman is beautiful and called by God to fulfill her God-given purpose in life (Proverbs 31).

She loves to pray, and you can find her on JJ Ministries' Prayer Line Monday–Saturday mornings, 5–6. The Word of God is her weapon, and prayer is the key to overcoming every obstacle in life. She loves reading, traveling, tennis, board games, meeting interesting people of different backgrounds, fellowshipping with the saints, and spending time with her family.

Follow her on social media:

Facebook: www.facebook.com/marlene.asseviero
Instagram: www.instagram.com/celeste4real/

Tanisa Newby

Tanisa S. Newby was born and raised in St. Andrew, Jamaica, and is the mother of three lovely children: two handsome sons and a beautiful daughter. Being the only girl in a family with four sons, she is strong and has learned to maneuver challenging parental situations.

Tanisa is a certified Newborn Care Specialist, with a background and training in Customer Service and Office Administration. Having over 10 years of professional experience in childcare, she loves and has worked with children of all ages. One of her long-term goals is to publish her own series of children books.

Tanisa considers herself a social person with a passion for helping anyone in need of support, especially single mothers and girls in unfortunate situations. She is working to establish an online support group that is geared toward mothers who are raising their children from a distance, including women who have had to leave their children with relatives in order to provide for their families. Her program would also serve teenagers who are missing their mothers and need emotional support to help them cope while their mothers are away.

As a woman of faith who believes in the love and grace of Jesus Christ, she believes in positive outcomes. She is resilient in overcoming obstacles and celebrates her triumphs. She does not believe in coincidences, and one of her favorite sayings is "Nothing happens by chance."

Follow her on social media:

Facebook: www.facebook.com/TanisaNewby

Irina Curenton

 Irina Curenton resides in Columbus, Ohio, with her handsome husband of 18 years and six strong sons, including a set of twins. Her passion is seeing families thrive. She is a Creative Visionary, purposeful Speaker, Author, Educator, Transformational Coach, and Entrepreneur.

Irina is called to heal and release parents and children from the wounds and scars that have been passed on through the generations, bridging the gap to assist in the rebuilding process and freeing mothers to walk in their authority. She educates families on how to restore peace in their homes and empowers women to HEAL from trauma and create sustainable habits to THRIVE beyond the nine-to-five!

While working with at-risk youth in a group home setting, Irina developed a burning desire to partner with parents to help their children succeed in life. Based on that desire, Irina founded Shining STARZ Learning & Development Center in 2008 to serve as a safe space for children ages 0–12 to grow and develop holistically. Her program has grown organically to include Family Empowerment Coaching, Kids Leadership Development, and Women's Healing and Accountability Coaching.

Irina shares the message of reconciliation and restoration through faith, hope, and love with her audience, and she'd love to connect with you. Allow Irina to inspire you to fully embrace your healing process, develop your voice, and break negative generational cycles and patterns.

Blog site: https://hopereconnects.com
Facebook: www.facebook.com/hopereconnects
Instagram: www.instagram.com/hopereconnects

Pamela Wilson

Pamela Wilson, a proud West Indian, is a Parent Coordinator with decades of experience working alongside students, adults, and families from all walks of life. Born in Kingston, Jamaica, she migrated to the States and has lived in Brooklyn for many years. Pamela specializes in providing resources for families in the school community. She is a powerful force in her sphere of influence and uses her positive attitude and tireless energy to encourage others to find and use the resources they need to succeed.

Pamela is inspired daily by her family, her three children, and her two granddaughters. In her free time, she likes to laugh, spend time with family, and make the most of her downtime. She aspires to be a writer and continues as a community activist, bringing light and sharing space to let people know that, no matter their background and story, they deserve to be heard.

Follow her on social media:

Facebook: www.facebook.com/pamela.wilson.7355

Acknowledgments

Jeremiah 29:11

"For I know the plans I have for you," declares the Lord, "plans to prosper you and not to harm you, plans to give you hope and a future."

The inspiration for this book came the same way as for my other books. I heard the voice of God, saying, "It's time for you to open your doors to the public and move to the next level with your publishing company." As always, I'm moved by God's confidence in me; but at the same time, I asked, "God, how many things do You want me to do at once?" God had given me a big job, and I did not want to disappoint him.

God instructed me to publish three anthology books this year (2021) and to birth entrepreneurs. To be honest, I told God that His plans were a lot to ask. But then, God reminded me of His words in Jeremiah 29:11: "For I know the plans I have for you,' declares the Lord, 'plans to prosper you and not to harm you, plans to give you hope and a future,'" and as a result, *The Secret Prayer of a Righteous Black Woman: The Power of a Mother's Prayer* was born. This is why my first acknowledgment goes to God, who is my inspiration behind all the work I do. In Habakkuk 2:2, the Word says, "Write the vision and make it plain on tablets, that he may run who reads it." God, I have done that which you've instructed me, and I thank you in advance for the blessing, and I pray that the peace of God, which transcends all understanding, will guard the hearts and minds of each reader.

In addition, I would like to give a special "Thank You" to all my **exceptional** co-authors—Fenyx Blue, Rhonda Small Peters, Michelle W. Fuqua, Debra Turner-Ray, Chandele Morris, Leslie Ann Jack, Deborah C. Carrington, Marlene Asseivero, Tanisa Newby, Irina Curenton, Pamela Wilson—for completely embracing the vision when it was introduced to you and for your willingness to share your stories, the contributing factors of this powerful anthology that we have created together.

What is an influential book without an equally powerful foreword? A special thank you to Dr. Janell Jones for your invaluable contribution to this anthology, you are genuinely appreciated. Your compelling words of wisdom will bring enlightenment to everyone who reads this book. In addition, I would also like to acknowledge Nzinga Fortune (my favorite cousin) for her thought-provoking and inspirational spoken word piece, which adds to the authenticity of this anthology.

As it relates to the creation of this book, I would like to extend a heartfelt thanks to my team. The most exceptional and well-known authors rely on qualified editors to enhance the quality of their manuscripts and proofread their work. In this regard, I would like to acknowledge Dara Powers Parker for her meticulous editing service and insight, which helped improve *The Secret Prayer of a Righteous Black Woman: The Power of a Mother's Prayer.* Your level of professionalism, customer service, and dedication provided me with editorial excellence. I would also like to give a special thanks to my illustrator, Alexandra Gold, for flawlessly recreating God's vision to me for this book cover and my graphic designer Kamaljeet Singh for doing an amazing job with the interior layout.

Finally, my family—my rock, my support system, and my muse. To my husband, Leon Rodney, and my three beautiful young-adult children: Denifa, Doreion, and Azal. You guys inspire me every day to persevere and to always believe in my dreams, because dreams really do come true.

NATIONAL CRISIS ORGANIZATIONS AND ASSISTANCE

Some of the serious issues discussed in this book include suicide, sexual assault, abuse, crime, alcoholism, and teen pregnancy. If you or a loved one is experiencing any of these or other crises, please consult the list below of organizations and hotlines. Whether you need urgent help, someone to talk to, or answers to questions, please don't hesitate to reach out.

Black Mental Health Alliance
(410) 338-2642
Provides information and resources and a "Find a Therapist" locator to connect with a culturally competent mental health professional

National Suicide Prevention Lifeline
1-800-273-8255 (TALK)
www.suicidepreventionlifeline.org

National Parent Helpline
1-855-4-A-PARENT (1-855-427-2736)
To get emotional support from a trained advocate, to become empowered to be a stronger parent

Parent Stress Line (Parents Helping Parents)
1-800-632-8188
Confidential and anonymous
Available 24 hours a day, 7 days a week

National Human Trafficking Resource Center/Polaris Project
Call: 1-888-373-7888 | Text: HELP to BeFree (233733)
www.polarisproject.org

National Child Abuse Hotline/Child Help
1-800-4-A-CHILD (1-800-422-4453)
www.childhelp.org

Teen Line (1-800-852-8336)
Operated by teens and gives other teens a resource for talking about tough life situations, including pregnancy

Hotline Number for Teens About Pregnancy
1-800-712-HELP
Geared toward teen girls and allows them to get answers to pregnancy-related questions

National Council on Alcoholism and Drug Dependence (NCADD)
1-800-NCA-CALL (622-2255)
Nationwide alcohol crisis hotline offers information, education, and hope to people with a drinking problem

National Institute on Drug Abuse (NIDA)
1-800-662-HELP (4357)
24-hour helpline dedicated to preventing substance abuse

National Sexual Assault Hotline
1-800-656-4673 (HOPE)
www.rainn.org

National Center for Victims of Crime
1-202-467-8700
www.victimsofcrime.org

JOIN OUR ANTHOLOGY SERIES
"NEVER LET A GOOD CRISIS GO TO WASTE." —WINSTON CHURCHILL

We are seeking **Motivated**, **Dynamic**, **Powerful**, and **Bold** Women and Men who are armed with a **SURVIVAL** or **INSPIRATIONAL** story. If this describes you, and you would like to share your story to empower and inspire others to discover their purpose and thrive, then join us. Our anthologies provide a full series of books that promote blessings in all areas, such as family, spiritual, mental, business, health, etc., and offer an incredible opportunity to help you monetize and leverage each book in the series.

To Learn More Visit

Website: www.darapublishing.co
Email: darapublishing@gmail.com
Website: https://darapublishing.co/coauthor-opportunity/
Email: coauthoropportunity@gmail.com

Follow Us on Our Social Media Platforms

Facebook: www.facebook.com/darapublishing
Twitter: https://mobile.twitter.com/darapublishing
Instagram: www.instagram.com/dara_publishing/

Notes

[1]National Institute on Alcohol Abuse and Alcoholism https://www.niaaa. nih.gov/publications/brochures-and-fact-sheets/alcohol-facts-and-statistics

[2]NCBI, National Library of Medicine, National Institutes of Health https:// www.ncbi.nlm.nih.gov/pmc/articles/PMC3758406/

[3]Center for Behavioral Health Statistics and Quality. (2019). 2018 National Survey on Drug Use and Health: Methodological summary and definitions. Retrieved from https://www.samhsa.gov/data/(a) Key Substance Use and Mental Health Indicators in the United States: Results from the 2018 National Survey on Drug Use and Health https://www.samhsa.gov/data/ sites/default/files/cbhsq-reports/NSDUHNationalFindingsReport2018/ NSDUHNationalFindingsReport2018.pdf(b) Alcohol and Drug Abuse Among African Americans https://americanaddictioncenters.org/ rehab-guide/addiction-statistics/african-americans (c) Substance Use Disorders in the African American Community https://www.naadac.org/ assets/2416/2020-06-10_suds_in_the_african_american_community_ webinarslides.pdf

Made in the USA
Middletown, DE
23 November 2021

53214883R00106